# MACABRE

**AN ART COLLECTION TO MAKE YOUR HAIR STAND ON END**

## The Best of 2013

Compiled by Lora Mercado

# MACABRE

## AN ART COLLECTION TO MAKE YOUR HAIR STAND ON END

## The Best of 2013

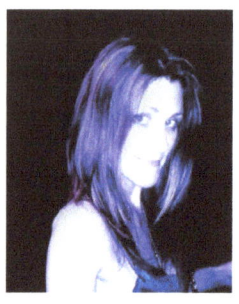

*Lora Mercado*
Founder/Editor

Dear Readers,

Welcome to Macabre Art Magazine - Best of 2013! I am very honored to feature the incredible artists and photographers who were kind enough to submit their works to me, to share with the world.

Each of these gifted artists and photographers give an original feel to their work.

Be sure to visit the artist's websites that are listed, to view more of their work.

Lora Mercado

ISBN: 978-0991026920

MacabreArtMagazine.com

# Diego Marcial Rios

**Diego Marcial Rios** lives in the San Francisco Bay Area and paints in acrylics. He graduated with honors with an M.A./M.F.A. from the University of Wisconsin at Madison, Department of Fine Arts Graduate School and a B.F.A. from University of California at Berkeley. Diego has a C.L.P. from the University of San Francisco. He received a number of fellowships for his Academic study. His artwork illustrates many complex social-economic issues faced by contemporary society.

Diego Marcial Rios' fine art has been included in more than 450 exhibitions from Japan to Bulgaria. He is in a number of Museum Collections: The Auchenbach Foundation Collection at the Palace of the Legion of Honor Museum in San Francisco, Coos Art Museum, Coos Bay, Oregon; Laguna Beach Museum, Laguna Beach, CA.; Museo National De La Estampa, Mexico City, Mexico, etc.

He has also illustrated a number of books and his work is part of a number of Public Collections: Harriet Taubman Gallery, MD; Mission Cultural Center, SF; Irish Arts Council, Belfast, Ireland and many more. He has appeared as a speaker on Art and been interviewed on Television and Radio. His artwork has been included in many magazines. Diego has been a recent guest speaker at UC Merced, St. Marys College, and San Jose State University.

diegomarcialrios.com

facebook.com/DiegoMarcialRios

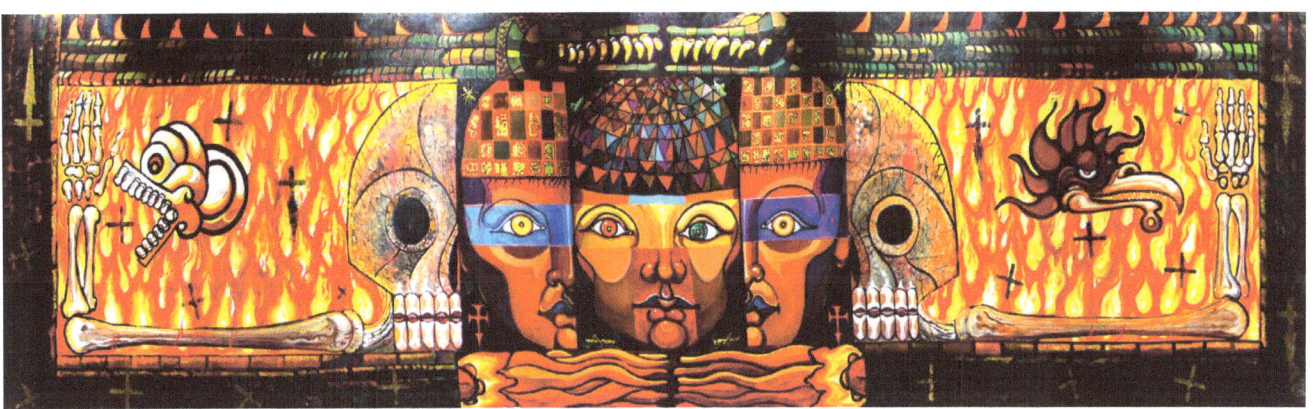

"Face of Life and Fire"
**Diego Marcial Rios**

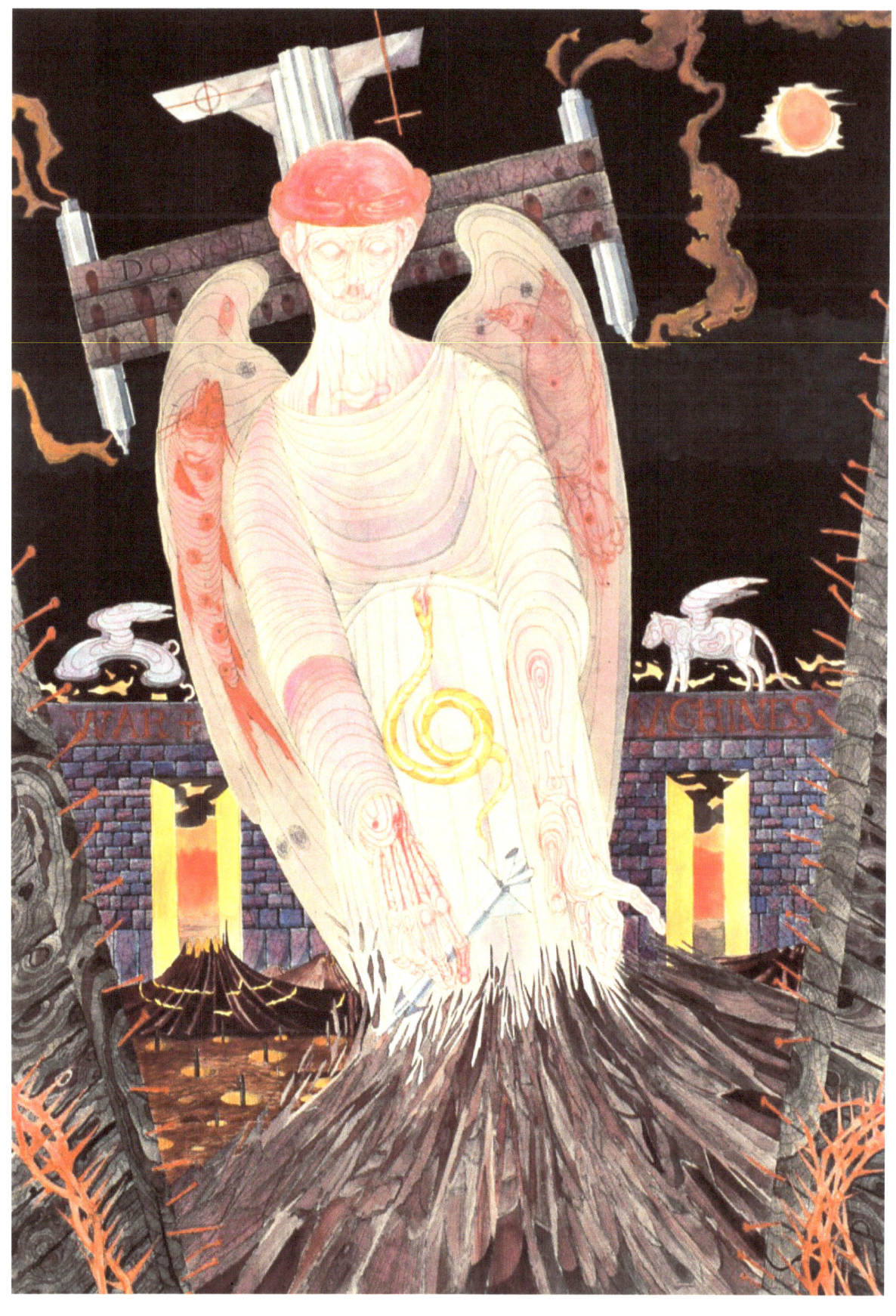

"Angel's Don't Dream War Machines"
Diego Marcial Rios

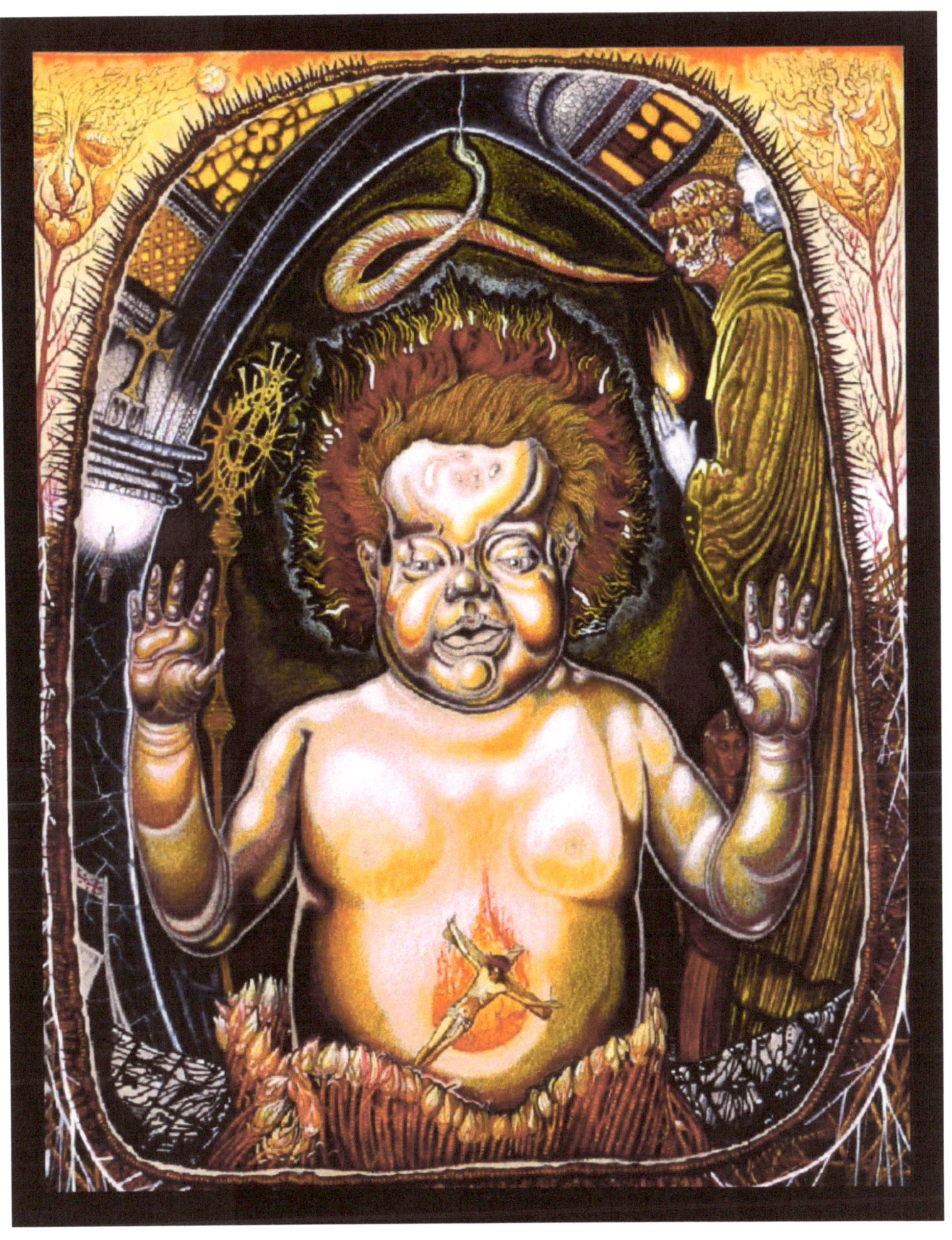

"Baptism"
Diego Marcial Rios

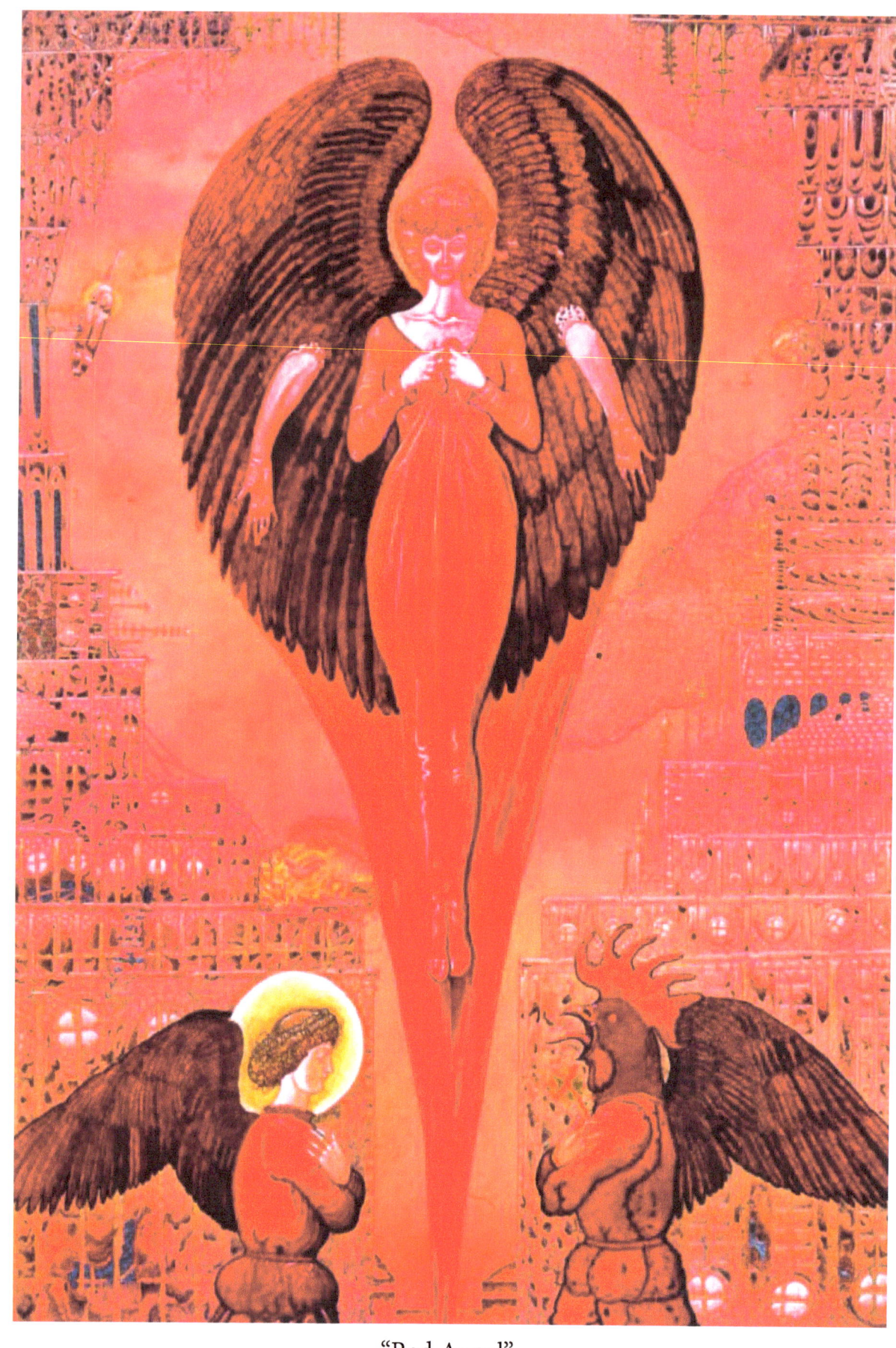

"Red Angel"
Diego Marcial Rios

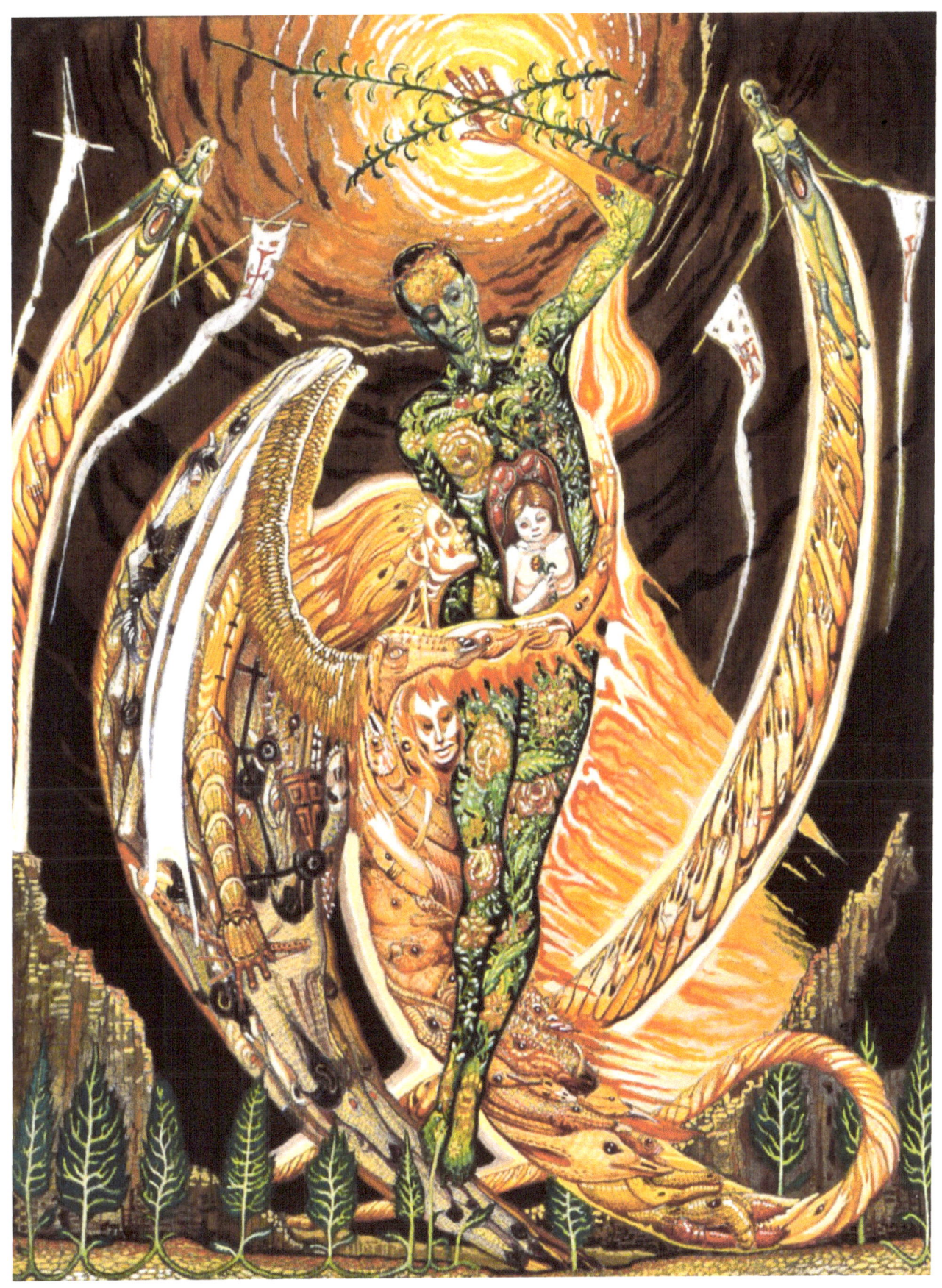

"Green Sleep"
Diego Marcial Rios

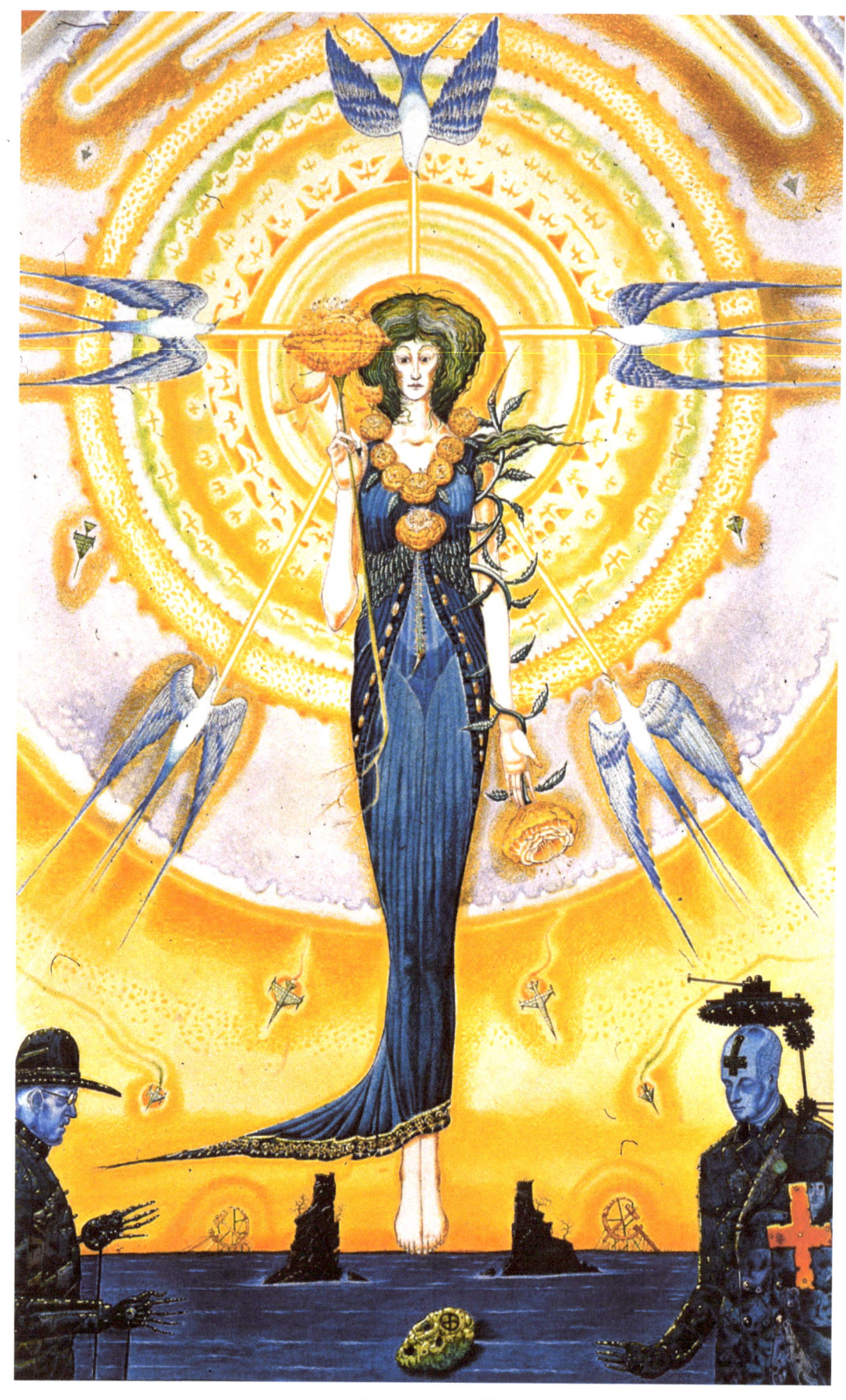

"Blue Angel"
Diego Marcial Rios

# Christopher Rehner

currently resides in his hometown of Johnstown PA, a small town near Pittsburgh, PA. He graduated from The Art Institute of Pittsburgh with a degree in Graphic Design and Fine Arts. Mostly working in Illustration, he utilizes Adobe Photoshop and Illustrator to give his work a more 'finished' look.

He has done work for many small businesses and different clients over the years, as well as illustrating his own comic book. Photo manipulation is something fun that he does with a lot of horror and pulp culture references being his inspiration, as well as a lot of artists that he admired growing up. The macabre and all things that go 'bump in the night' have always interested Christopher, since watching his first Zombie movie at age eight. A lot of his work reflects the dark and scary parts of man's subconscious. He loves doing a piece that makes someone question it, or have a feeling of being scared or disturbed, because that shows that he has done his job as an artist to invoke feelings in people.

Working with different companies made him realize to get the most from his talents, he needed to go out on his own. Christopher started a small in-house studio in his home called Zombie Kitten Designs ,a year and a half ago, to be able to do the type of work for people that he feels fits both himself and his clients.

**Christopher Rehner can be found on:** Facebook and DeviantArt.com

Mr.blix1979@gmail.com

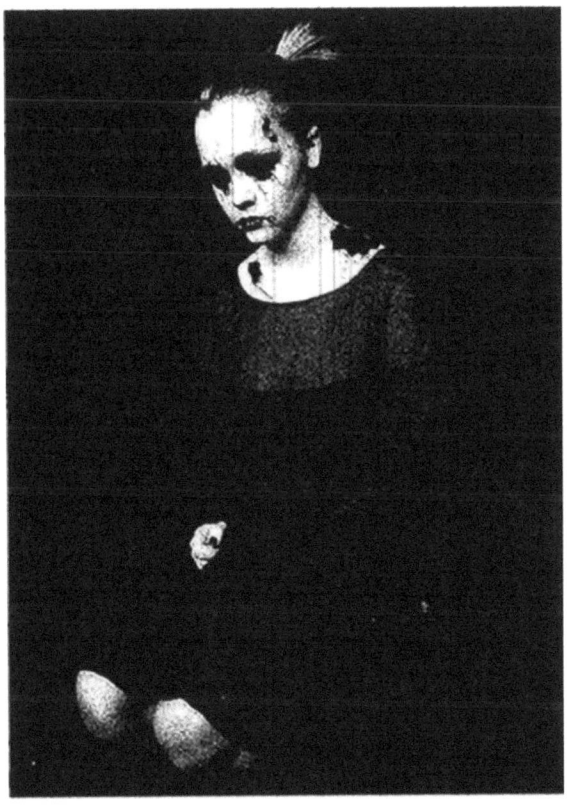

"Hopelessness"
Christopher Rehner

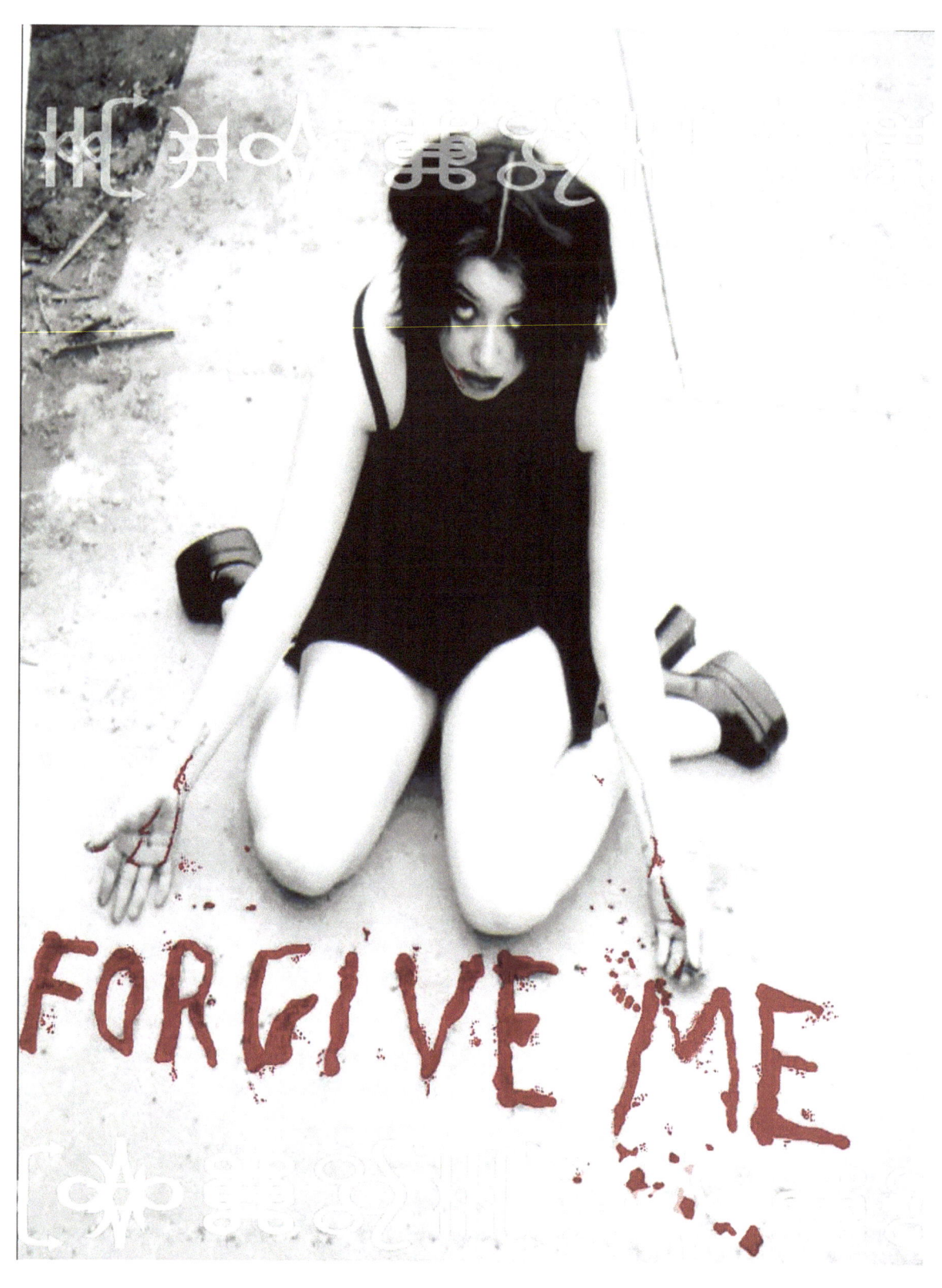

"Forgiveness"
Christopher Rehner

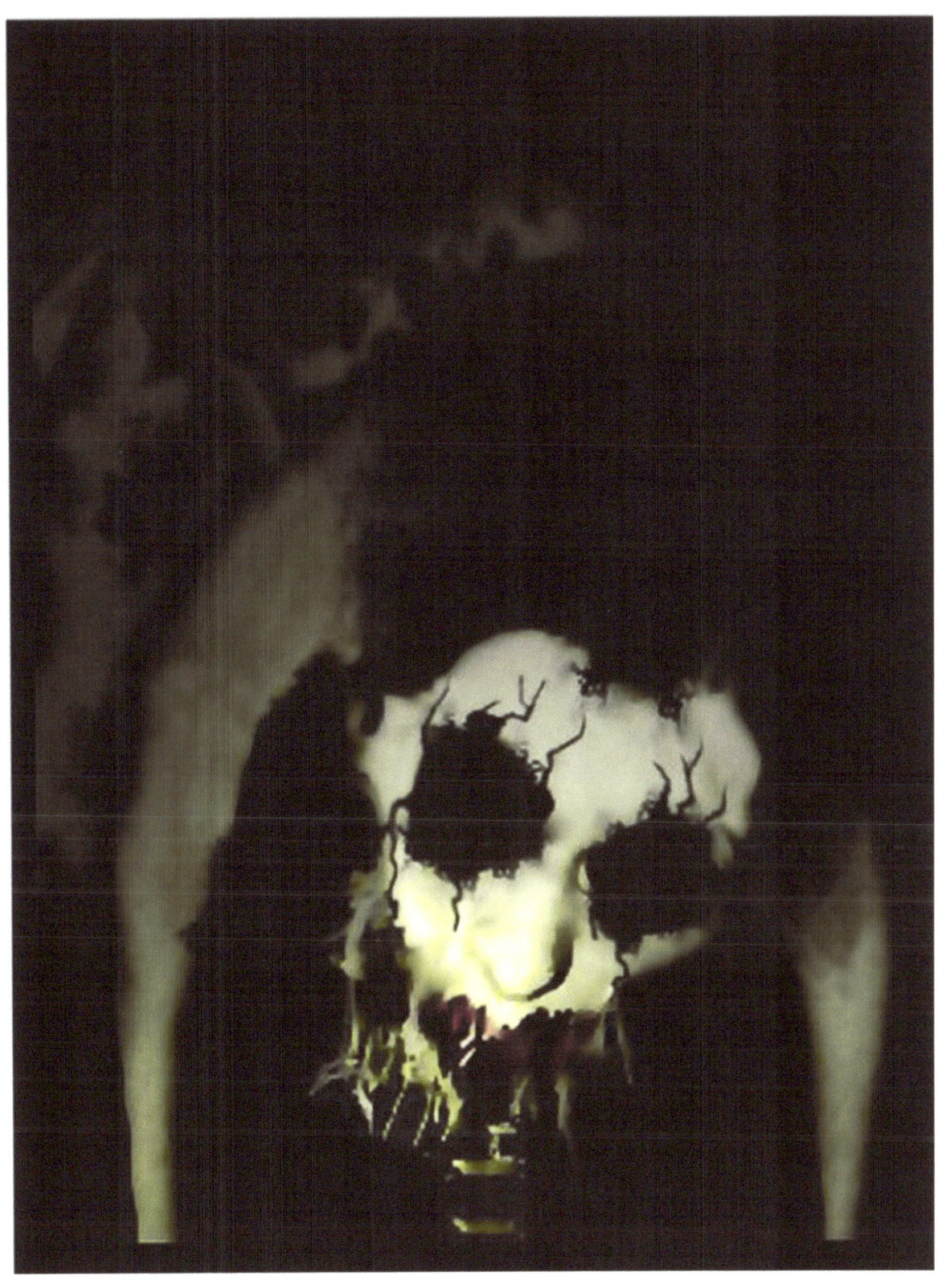

"Melancholy Suicide"
Christopher Rehner

# Joe Mays

is a photographer living and working in Louisville, KY. He loves photography of all sorts but for the past several years his continuing fascination has been with the human form and the way we can see new things about our fellow human beings by changing the lighting or context of the image.

His work has been displayed in shows in Indiana, Kentucky, New York and elsewhere. A current show containing a retrospective of all Mr. Mays' works is currently on display at OPEN gallery in Louisville, KY through April 20, 2013

alientwilight.com
joe.mays@alientwilight.com

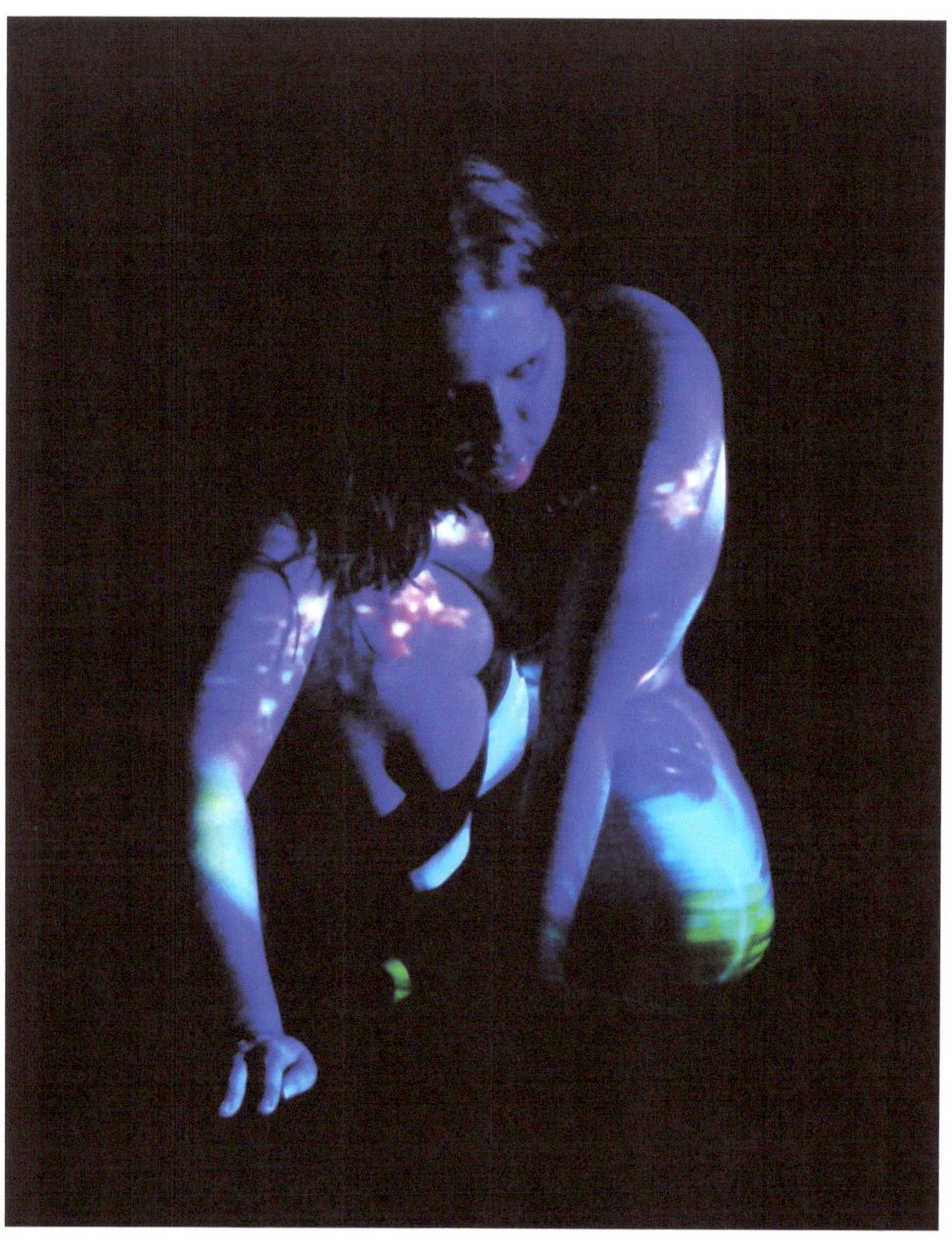

"Rest Uneasy"
Joe Mays

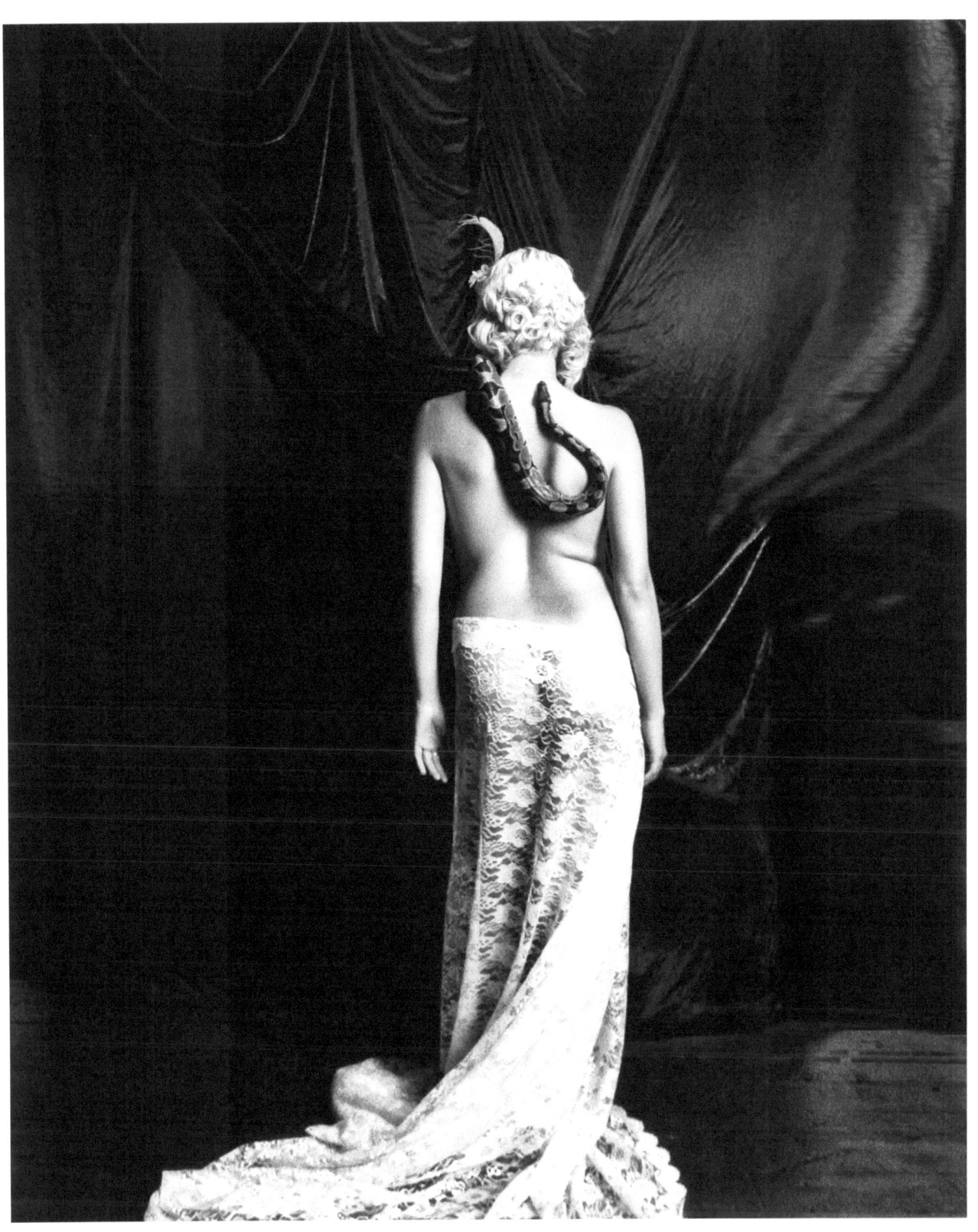

"Berlin Salon #6"
Joe Mays

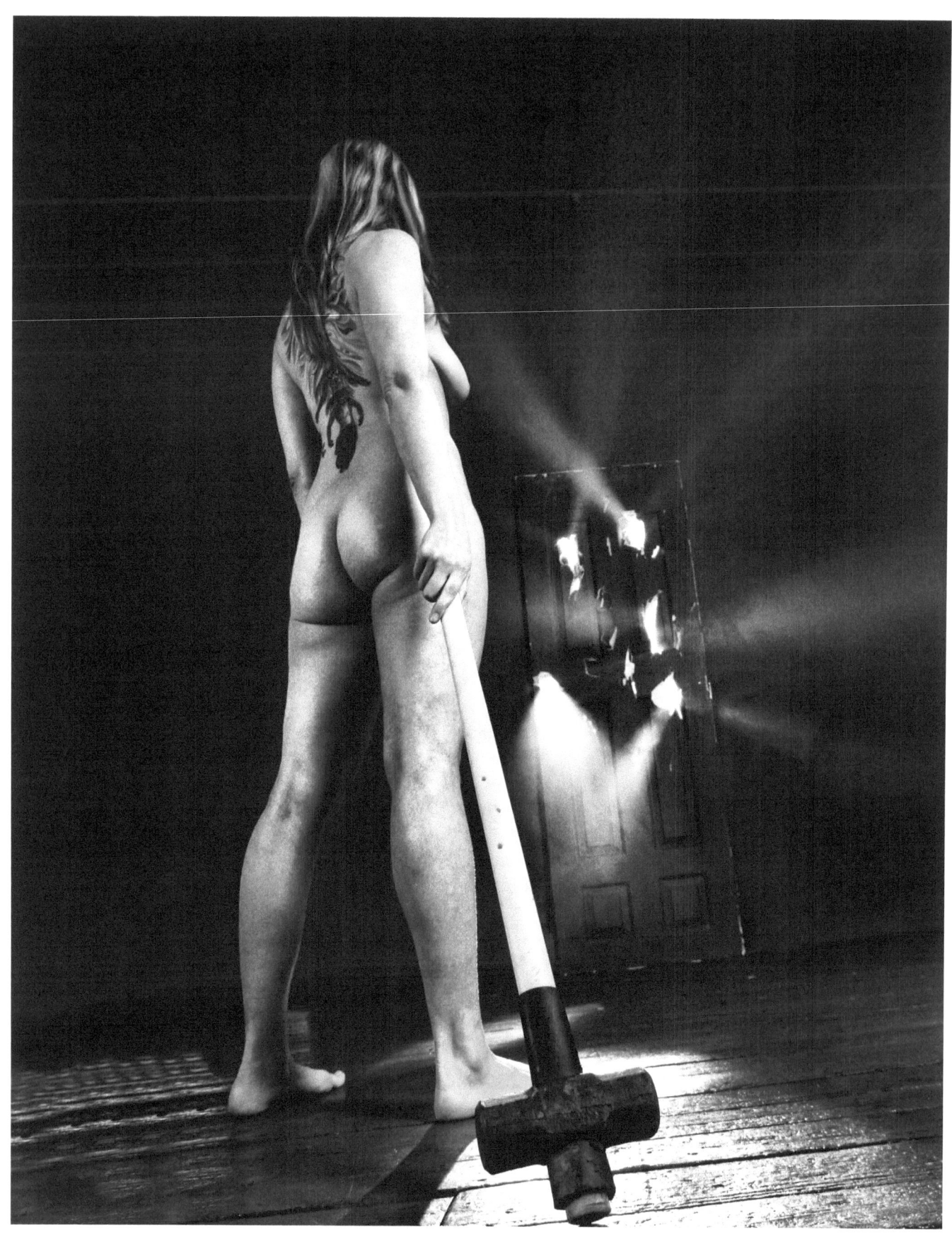

"Door #7"
Joe Mays

**Caitlyn Shea** uses paint to deconstruct and explore human and animal bodies. Her love for the unpredictable nature of paint and strong interest in anatomy guides her to work in an improvisational manner. Her subjects challenge the restrictions of having a perishable body.

After attending Pratt Institute and Skidmore College, Shea graduated from Adelphi University in 2011 with a BFA. Upon graduating she received an A. Conger Goodyear Award for Outstanding Artistic Achievement and a Senior Thesis Merit Award. She currently lives, works, and exhibits her paintings in New York.

caitlynartist.blogspot.com
caitlynartist@gmail.com

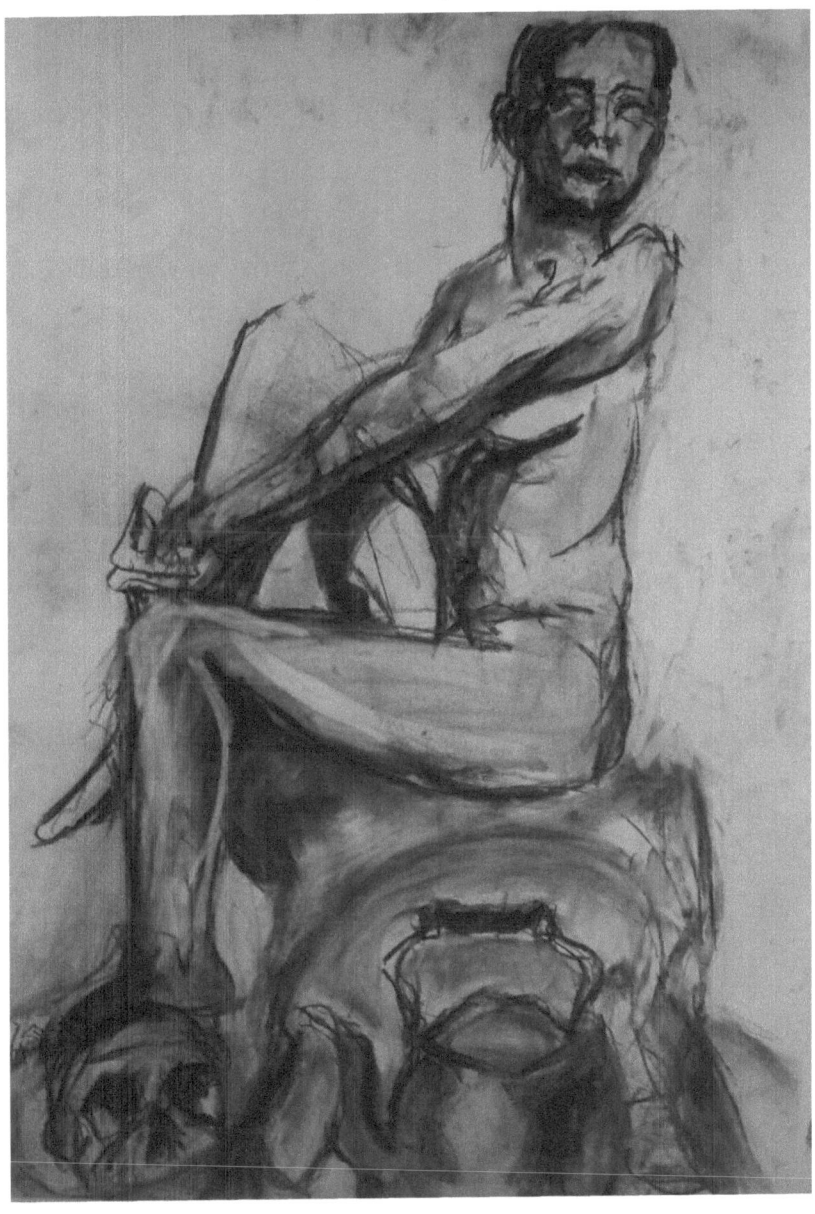

"Skull and Kettle"
Caitlyn Shea

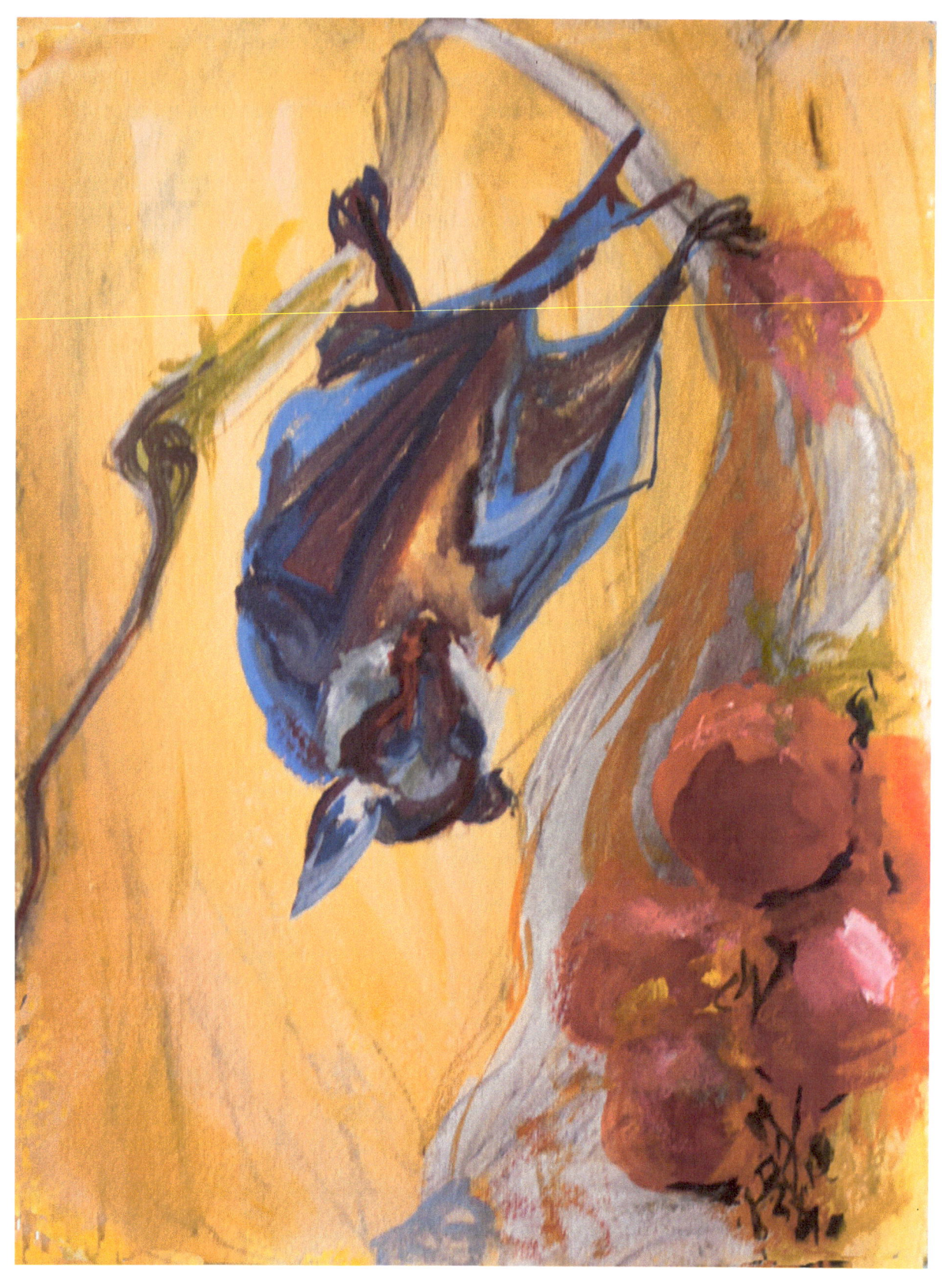

"Fruit Finder"
Caitlyn Shea

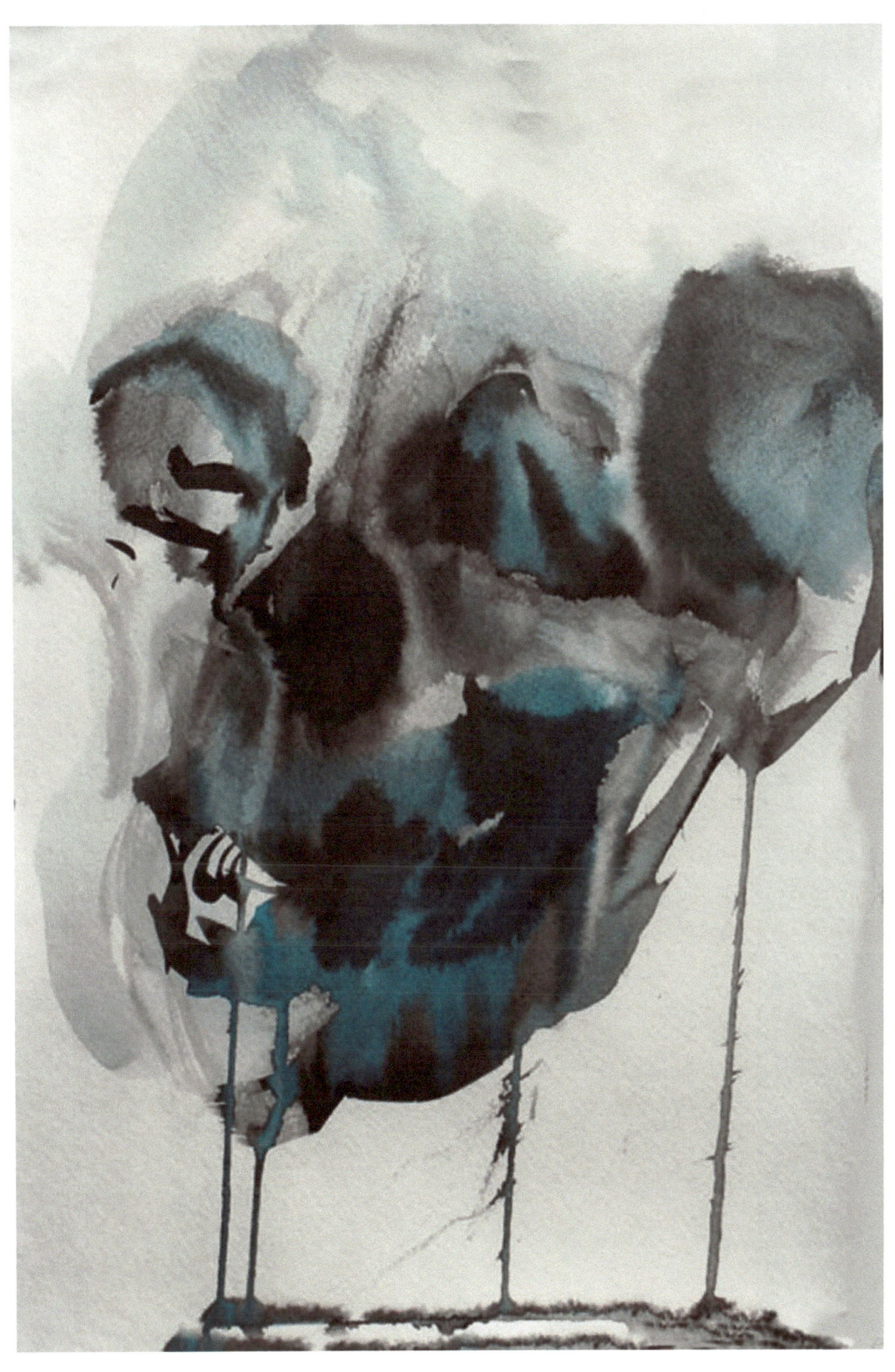

"Blue Remains"
Caitlyn Shea

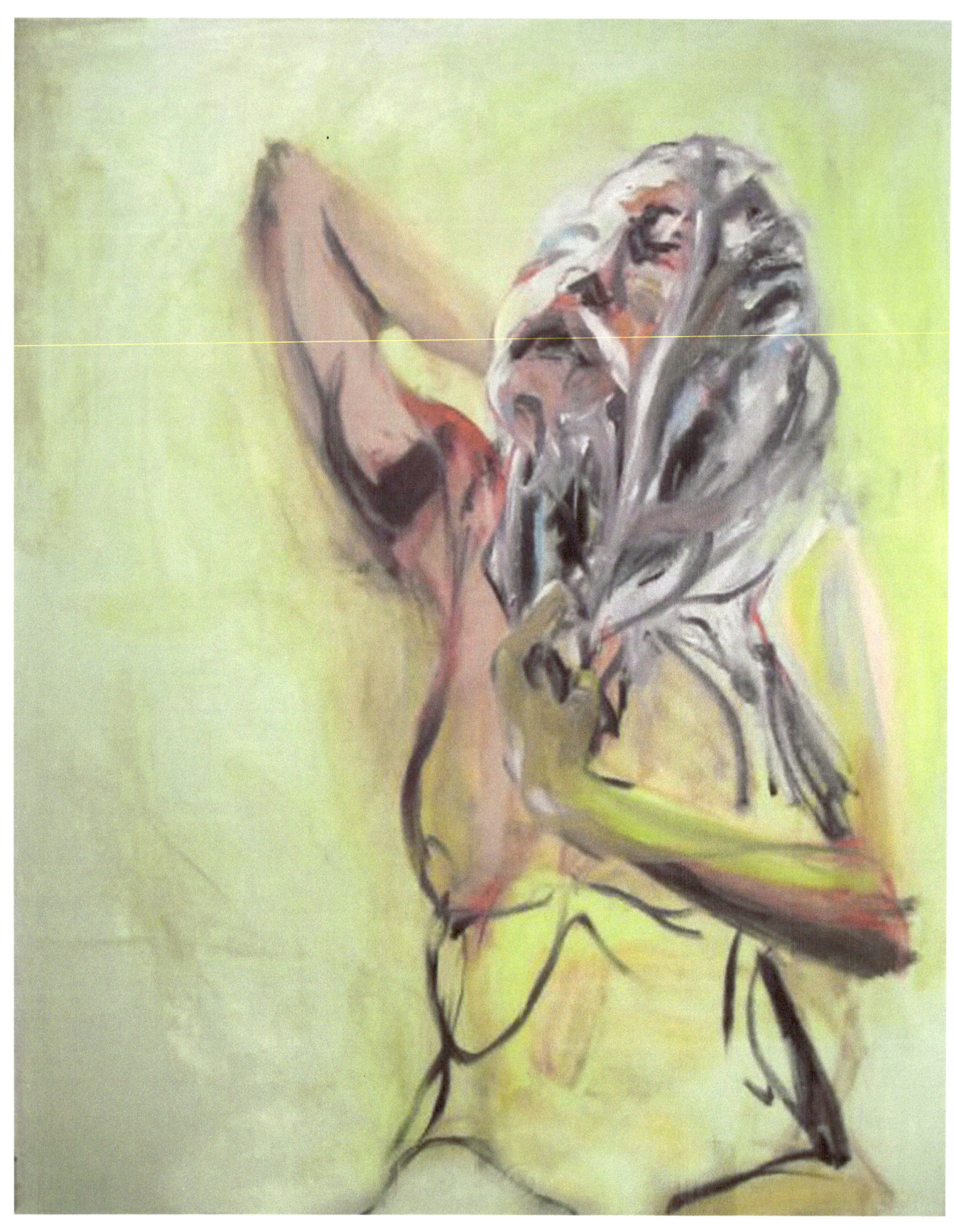

"The Long Endless Veil"
Caitlyn Shea

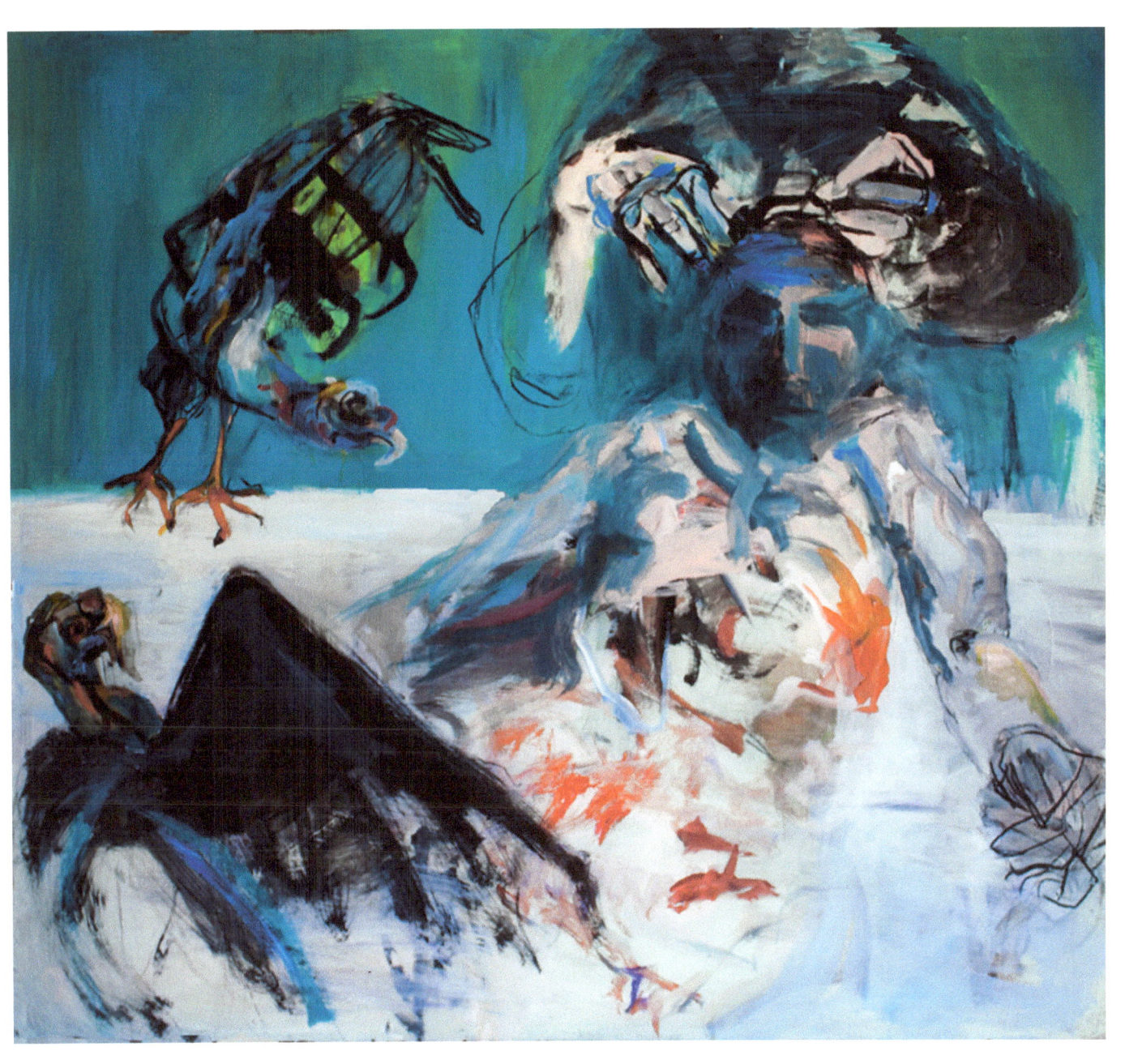

"An Anatomy Lesson for Vultures"
Caitlyn Shea

# Donna Abbate

There is an ancient belief that the language of birds is mystical, angelic or divine. Donna Abbate weaves this belief into contemporary Christian based imagery in hopes that symbiotic association between animal spirituality and humanity evolves. The surrealism is within that dream world of religion and primeval mythology.

In this way, she plays the mad scientist with art. A surrealist at heart, Donna juxtapose forms based on nature, known and unknown, microscopic and macroscopic. Her artwork is an orchestration of chaos; colors, shapes, plants, landscapes, animals, figures, collected and layered into a two dimensional spirit.

Like a spirit, each piece has a sense of self; a stately portrait, a dreamlike landscape or a scientific study of flora, infused with a vital force that challenges the veil of reality. These illustrations become, for Donna Abbate, a way to celebrate the mysterious and fantastic elements of our planet, asking the viewer to look again at their surroundings and contemplate the way things could be if there were no limits on our natural world.

www.abbateart.com

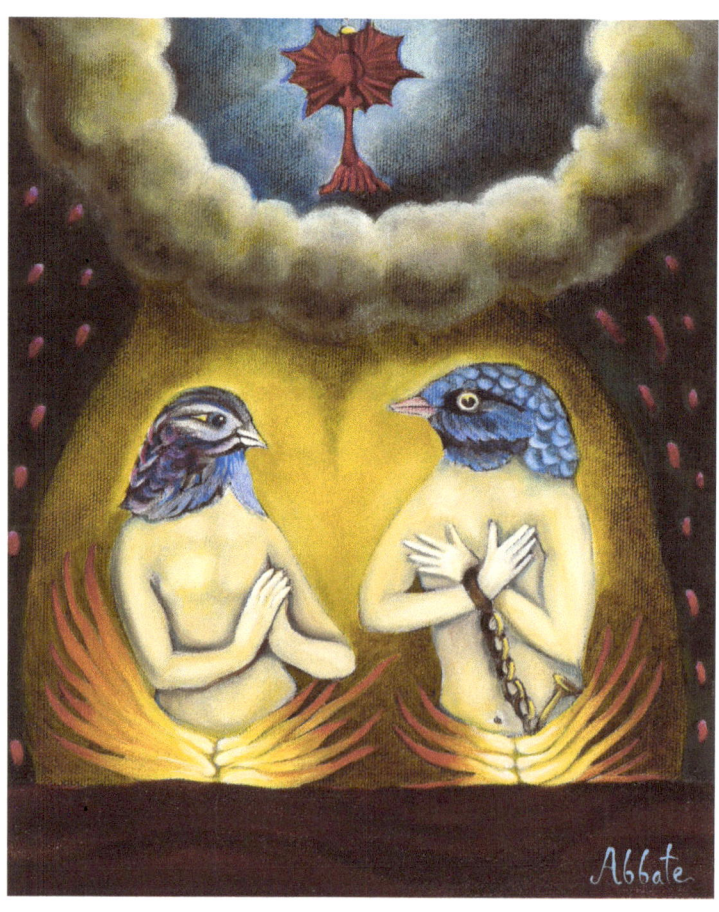

"Birds of Pray - Souls in Purgatory"
Donna Abbate

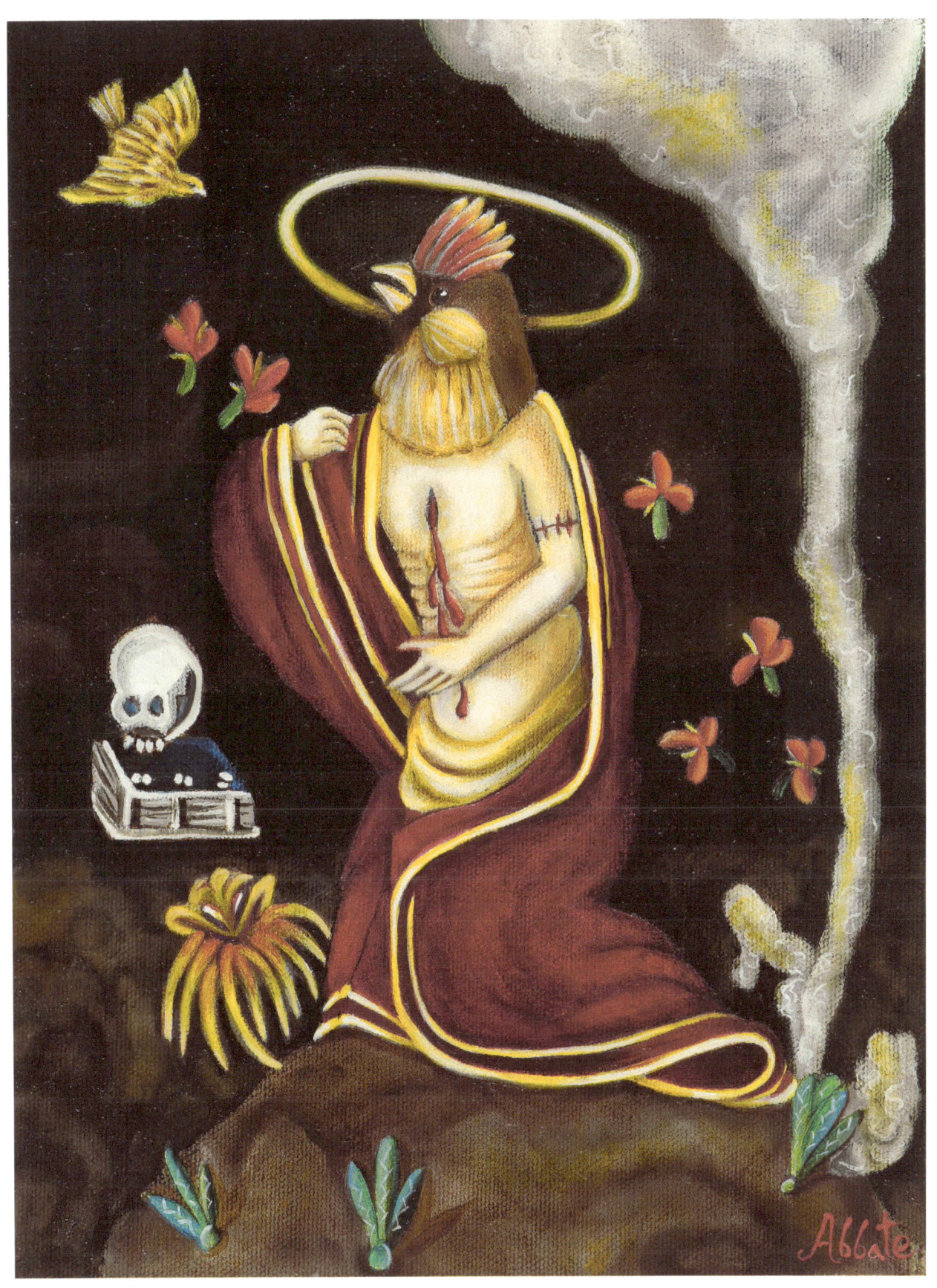

"Birds of Pray - Saint Jerome"
Donna Abbate

# Todd Petersen

has a day job as a professional photo retoucher and color technician for a printer in South Bend, Indiana. He spends his days working on images of dream kitchens and bathrooms far different than the ones found in the 150-year-old farmhouse in which he resides. Prior to his current position, Todd logged over 15 years in the publishing industry, both as a prepress technician and a book cover designer.

Todd's interest in photography really began while working as an art director for a cookbook company, when he provided art direction for several cover shoots. It was there that he learned what occurs on the other end of the lens. Soon, he was shooting in his own backyard, capturing a nest full of robins, some really bizarre caterpillars and lots and lots of flowers. For Todd, the camera part of it was the low point--the real fun began in post-production. However, a promotion to a "real" camera, with much better capabilities, has changed his mind considerably. Not one to shy away from challenging locations, Todd has been known to brave bitter temps if Lake Michigan's waves beckon on a blustery day.

etsy.com/shop/sharpeyephotography
coroflot.com/tdp
tdpetersen66@gmail.com

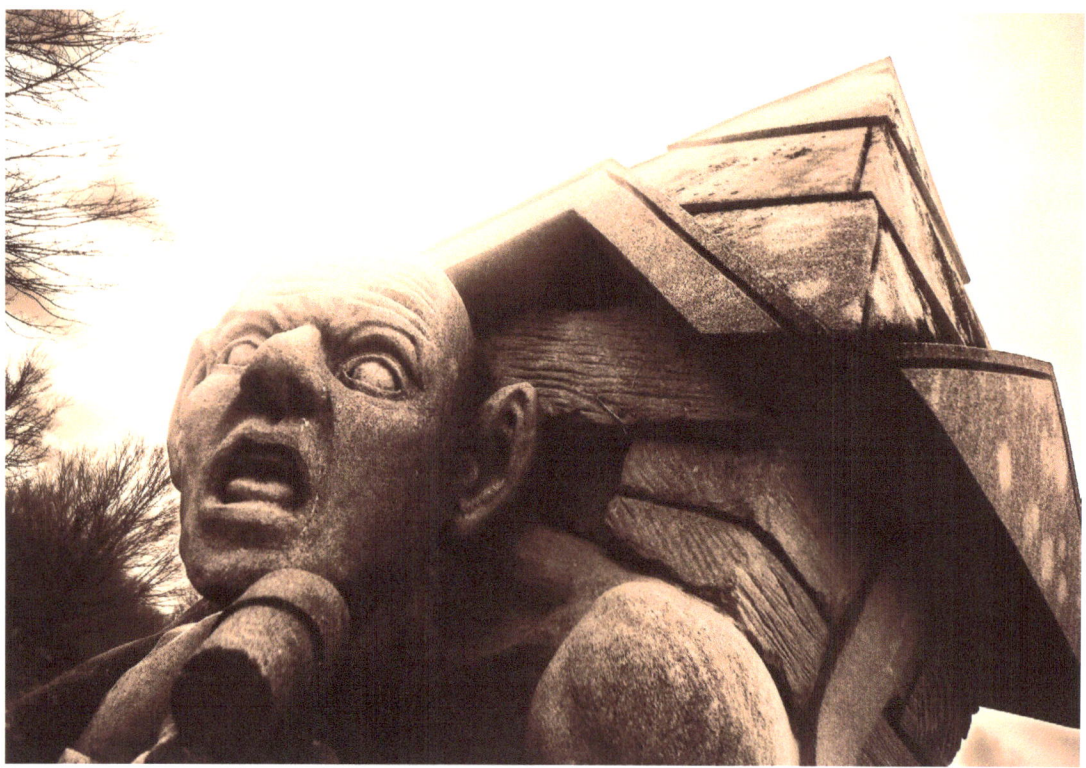

"Goblin"
Todd Petersen

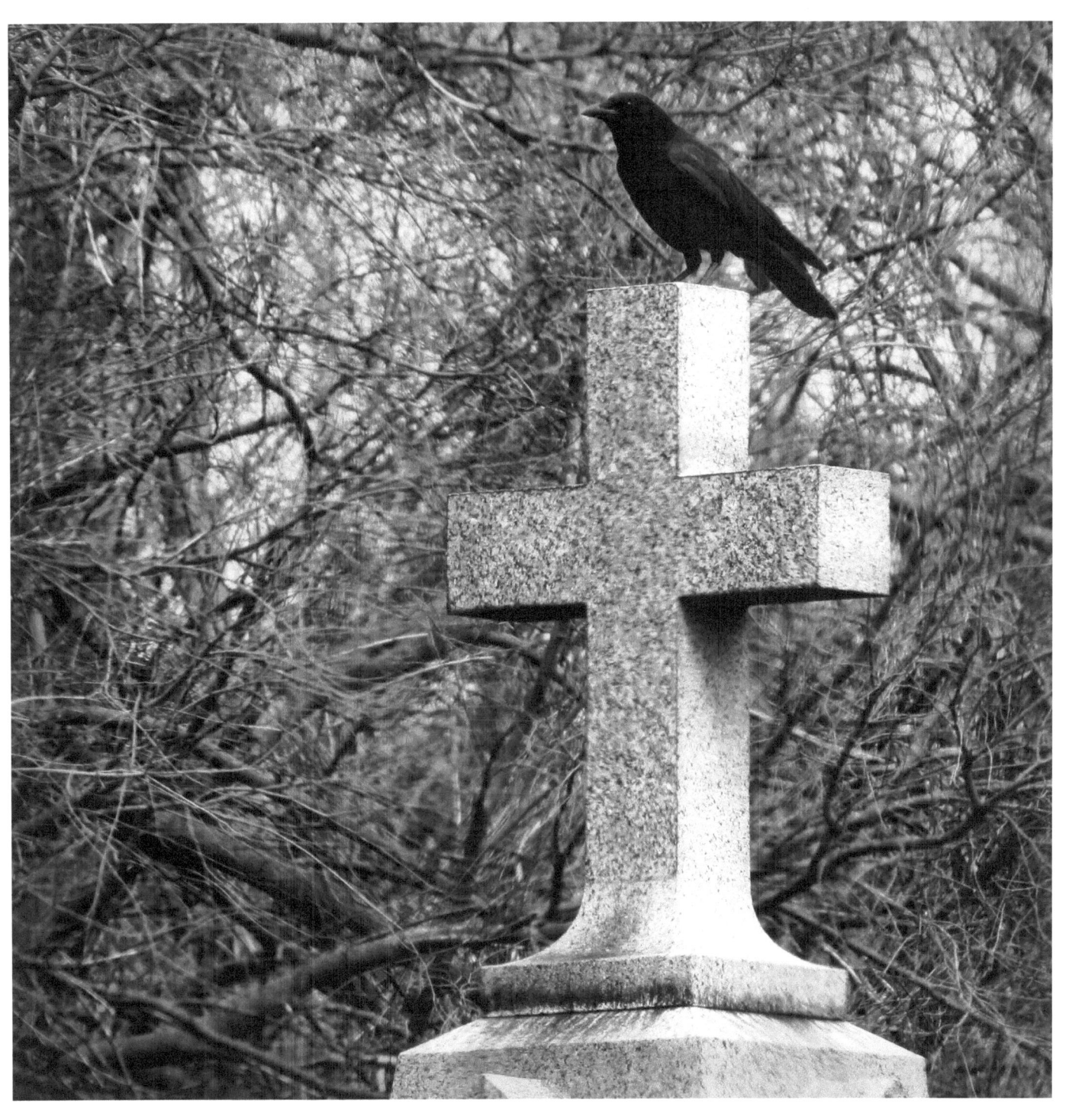

"Black Bird Watching"
Todd Petersen

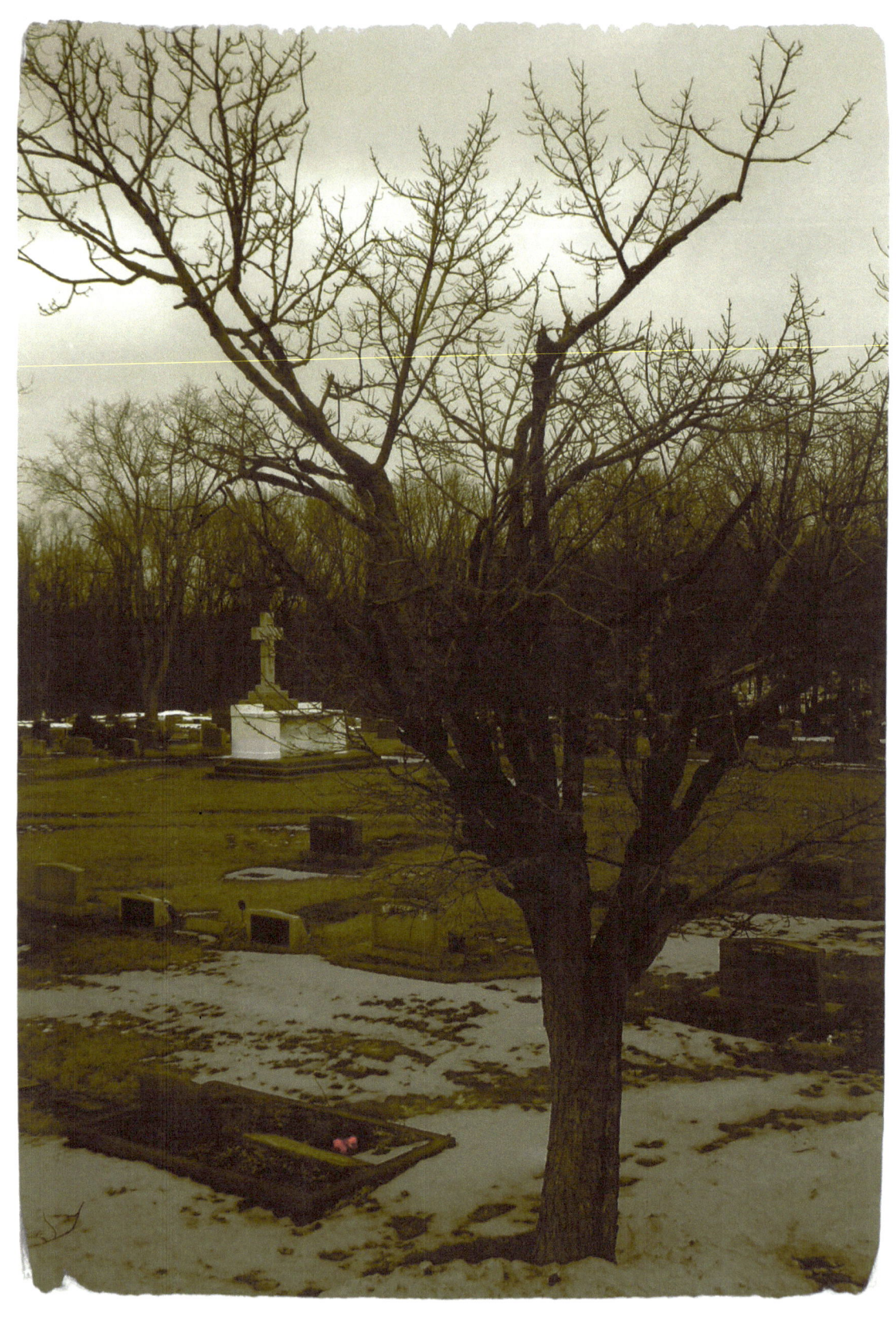

"Red Flower"
Todd Petersen

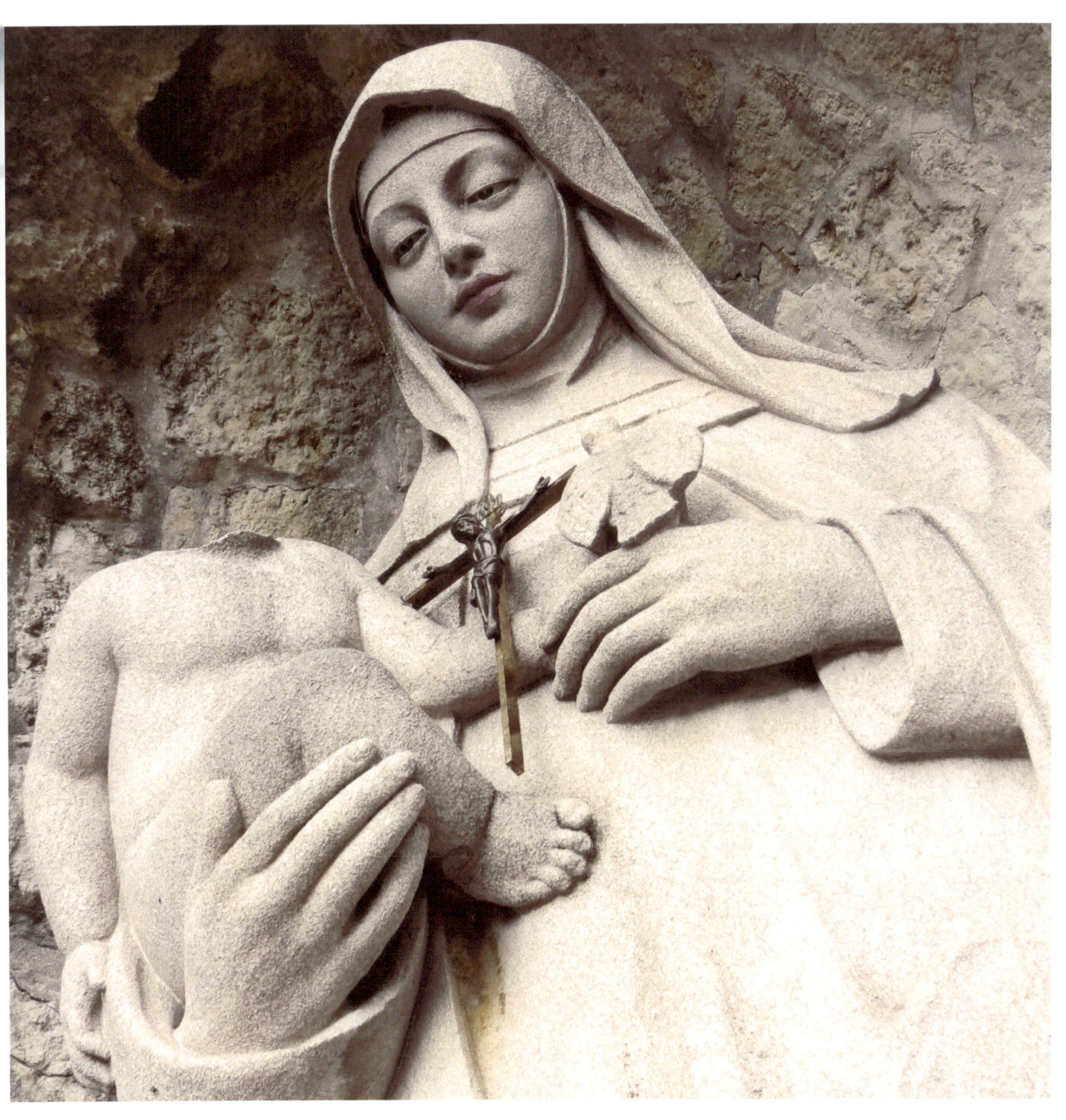

"The Look of Scorn"
Todd Petersen

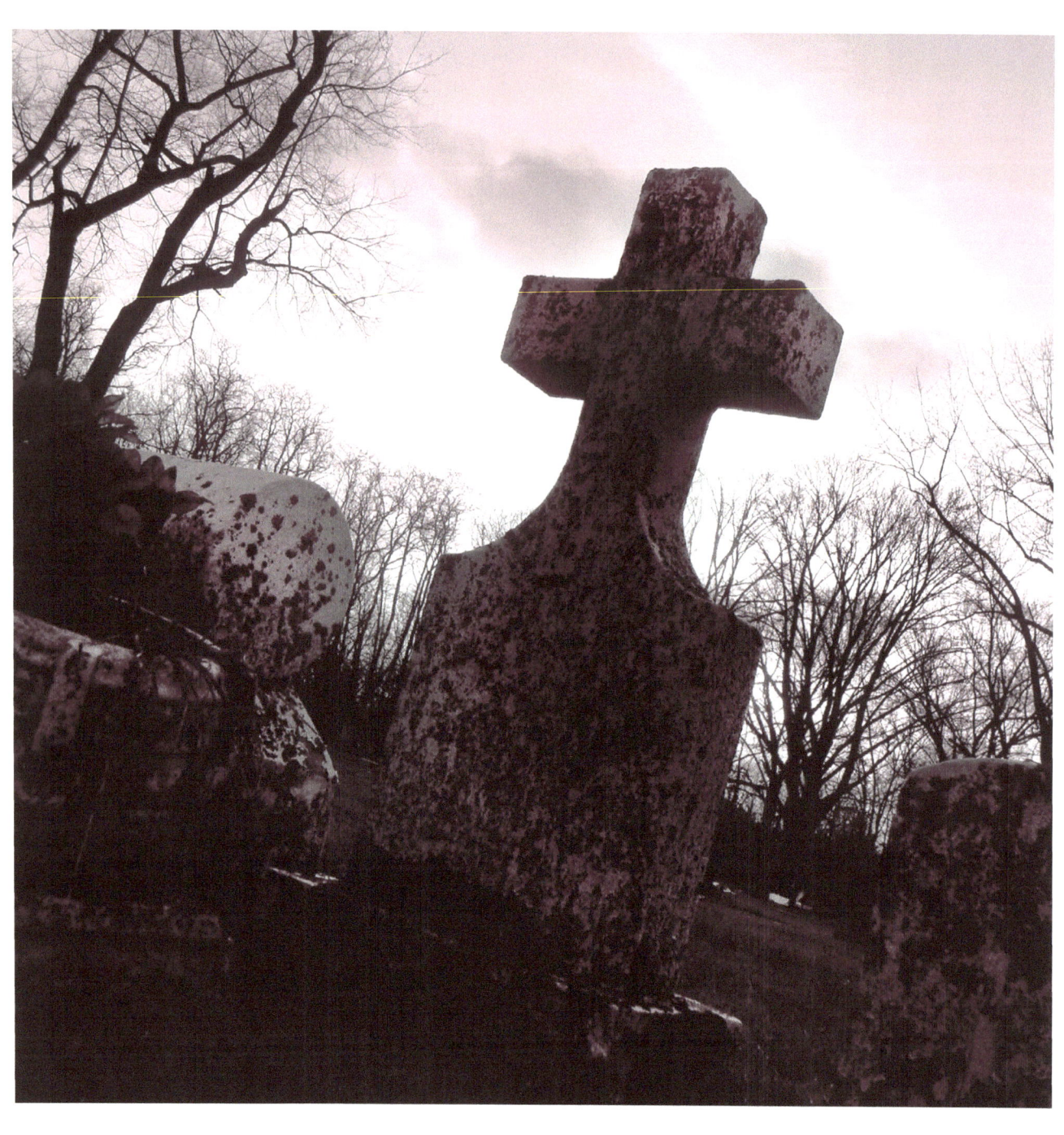

"Cross"
Todd Petersen

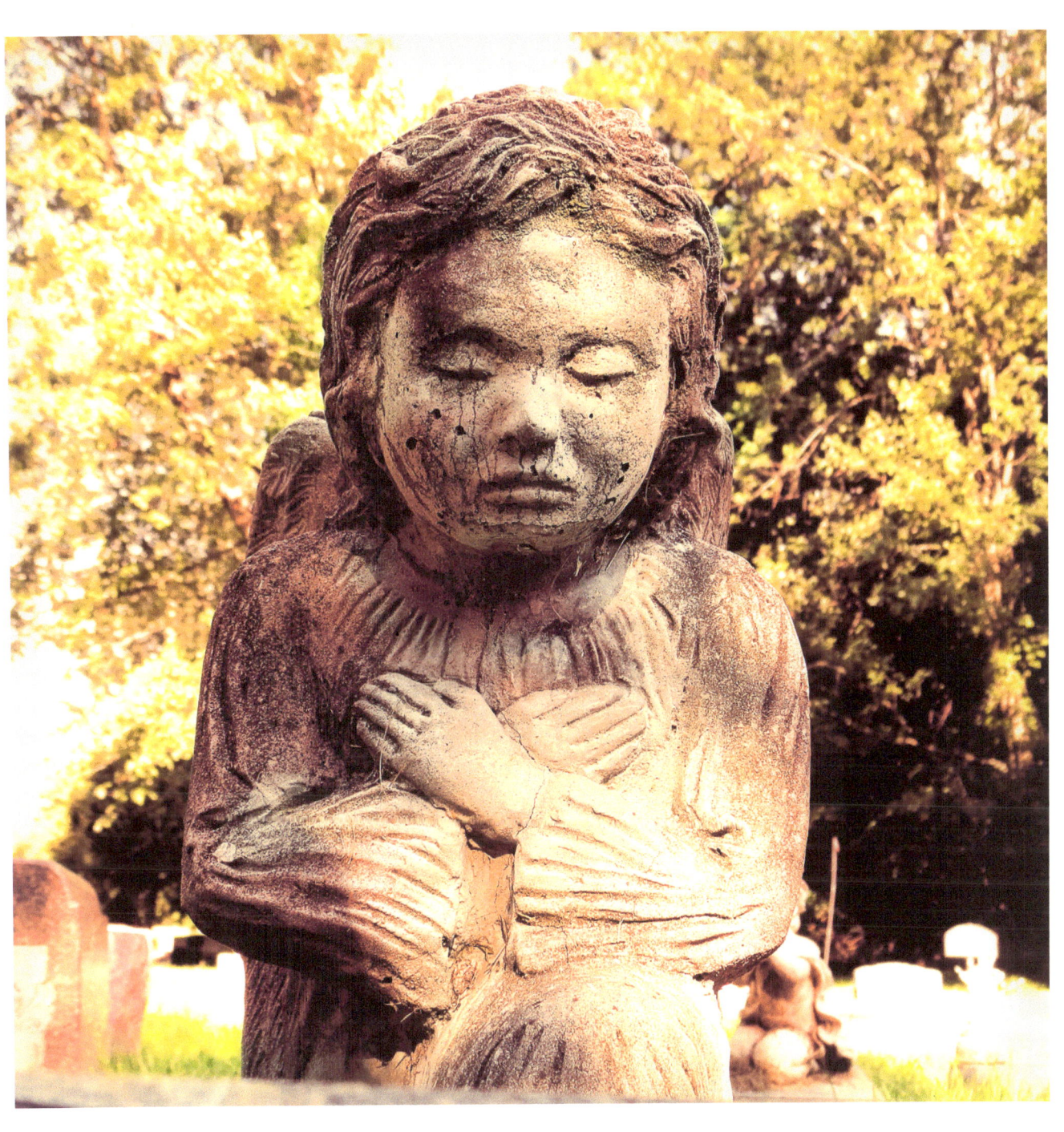

"Ever Flowing Tears"
Todd Petersen

# Juan Ramiro Torres

According to the Greek painter Omiros (1927-2010) "All paintings are essentially a self-portrait" and the painting of Juan Ramiro Torres agrees with the master, because through his work the artist recreates scenes or characters linked with his past or present that have made him the man he is.

"Knower of a glorious past, he throws the influence that the past plays in his creative spirit and manifests it in a present day form with a personal identity. Proof of that is in his series titled 'Lord of Sipan' and 'Inca Icons' or 'Iconoclasm', they show a marked influence of the Incas." (Maximo Anchea Castro, editor of Punto Hispano newspaper in Atlanta, Georgia).

Born in Lima, Peru Ramiro resides in the United States since 1984 where he studied Graphic Design and Illustration at the Parsons School of Design in New York City.

ramirin2005@hotmail.com
juanramirotorres.webs.com

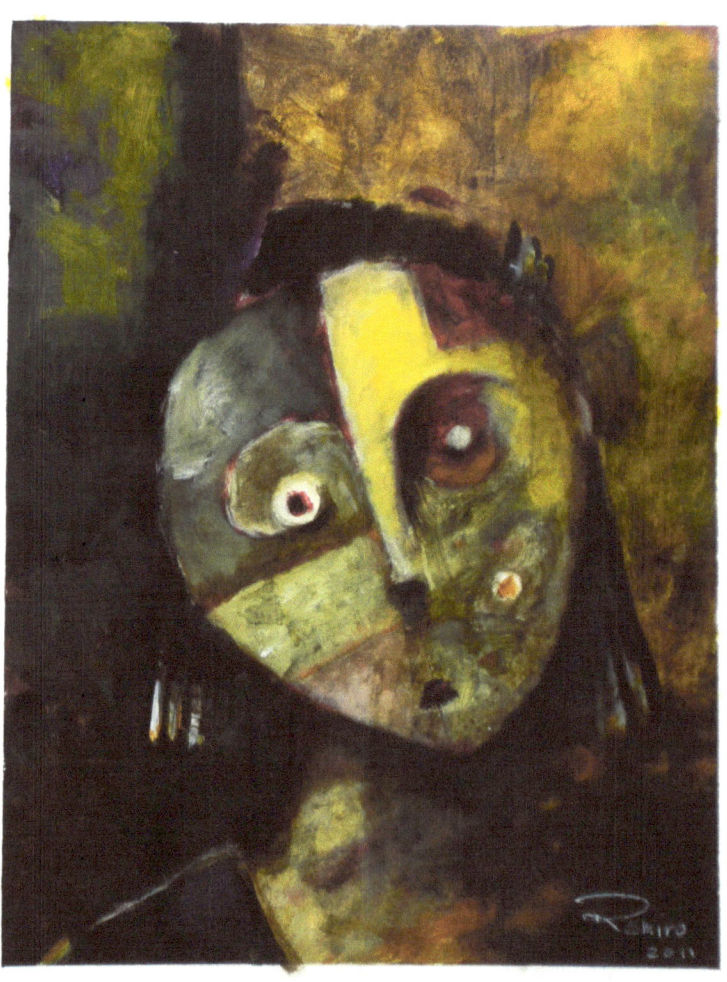

"Self"
Juan Ramiro Torres

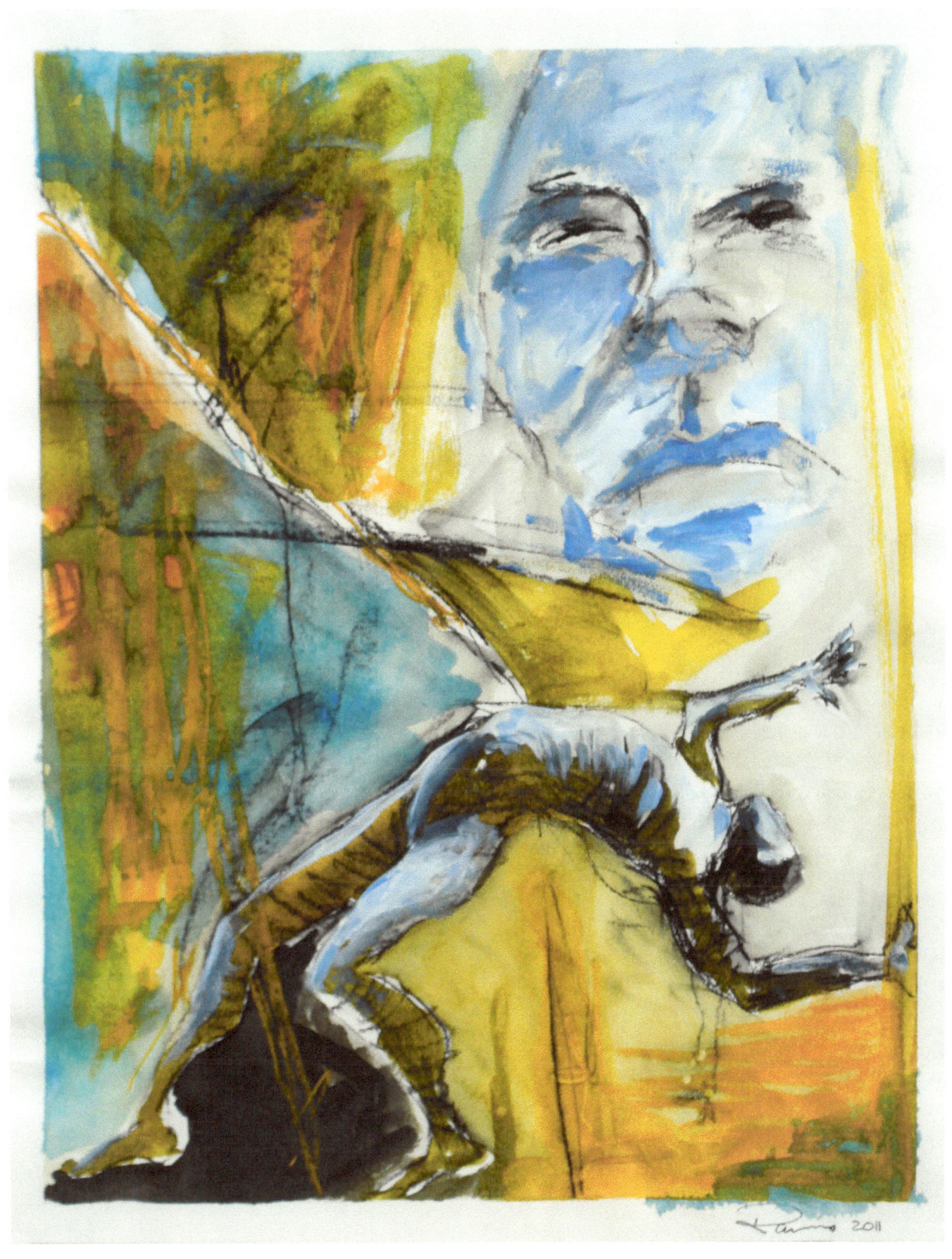

"Falling"
Juan Ramiro Torres

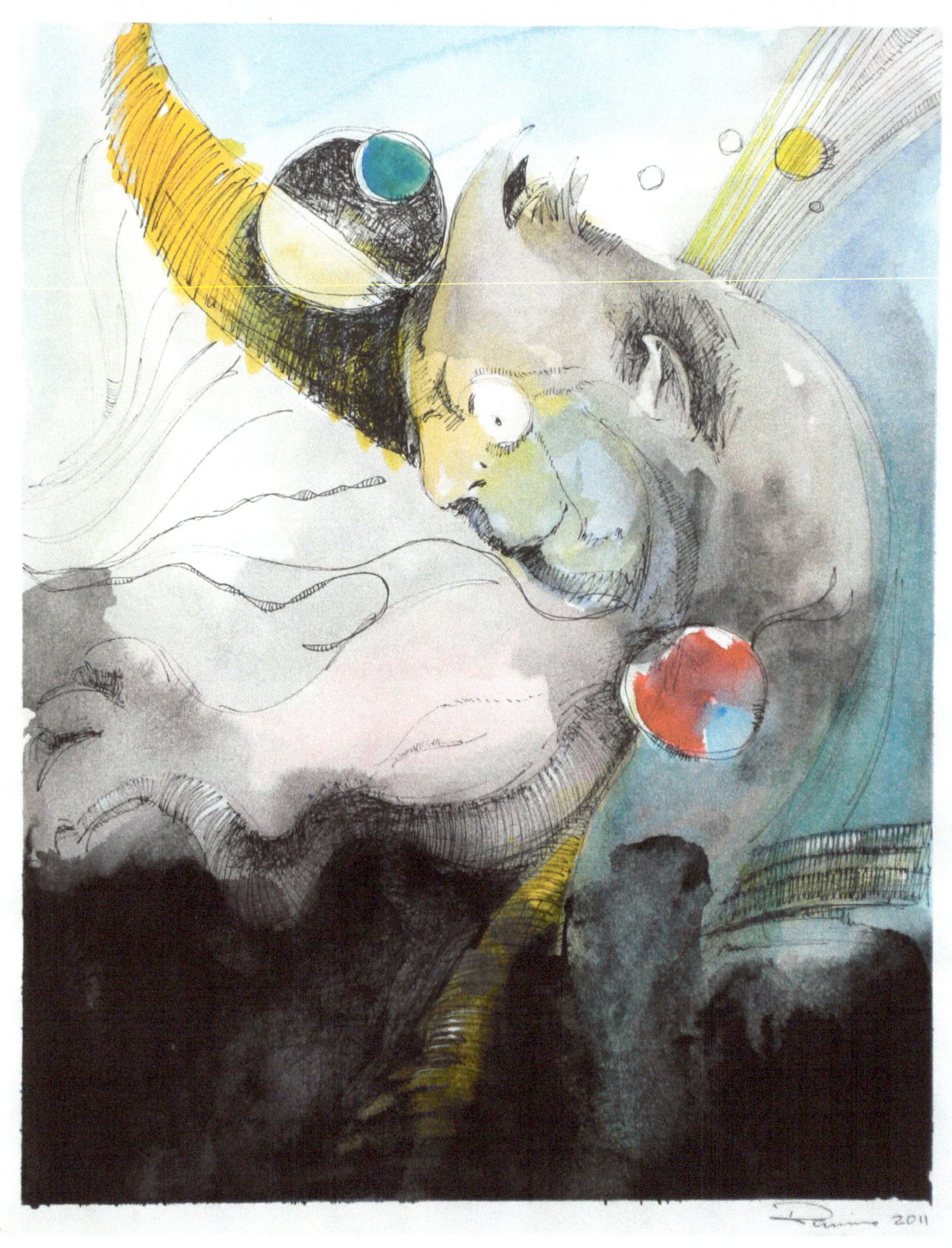

"Inside Demon"
Juan Ramiro Torres

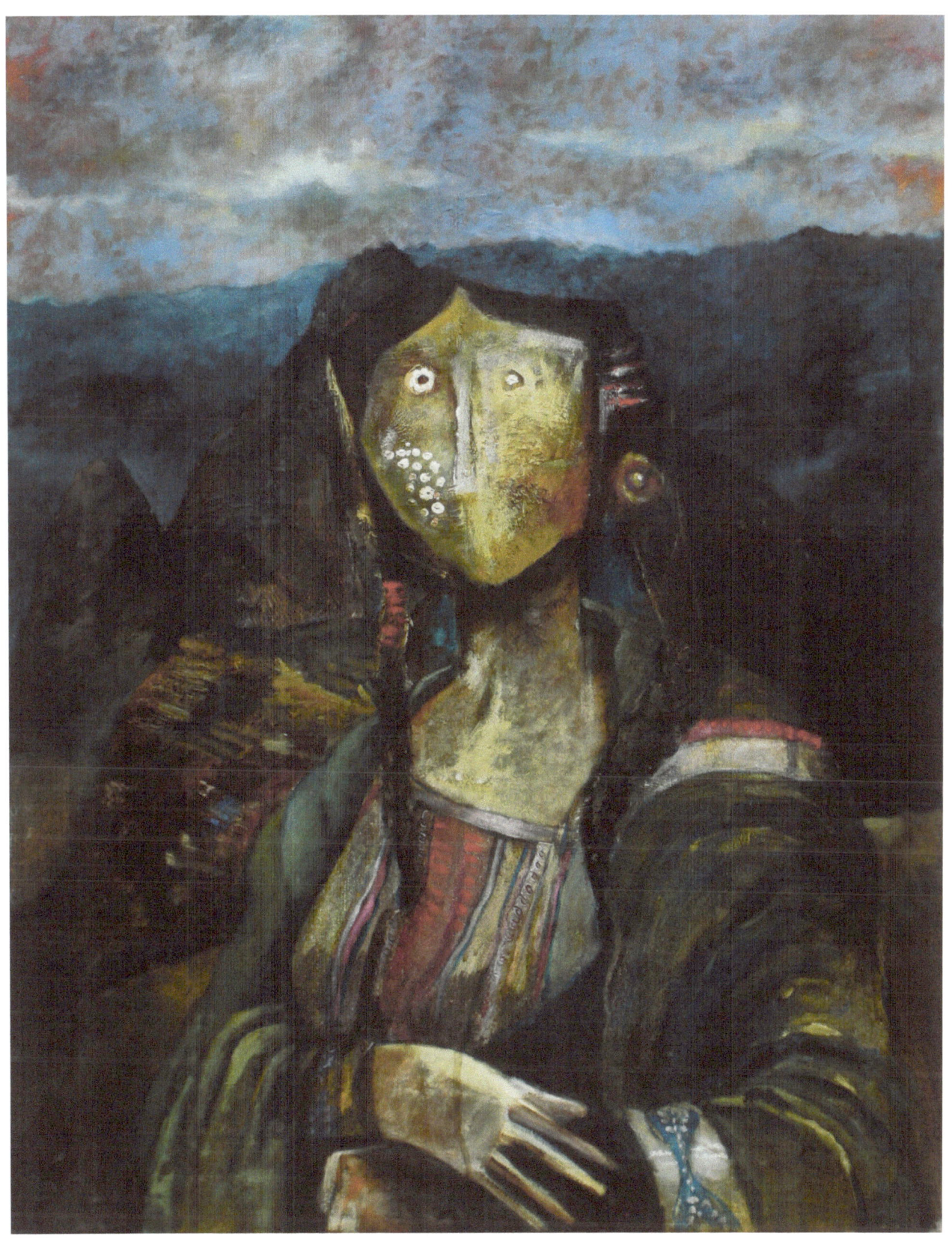

"Monalisa"
Juan Ramiro Torres

**Mary McVicker** is a truly passionate photographer. She loves nothing more than taking unique and eye-catching pictures that she can share with the rest of the world. Each photograph has a different meaning to everyone who views it, and she strives to challenge your perceptions and interpretations with every click of the shutter.

Facebook: Photography by Mary McVicker

mcvickerphotography@yahoo.com

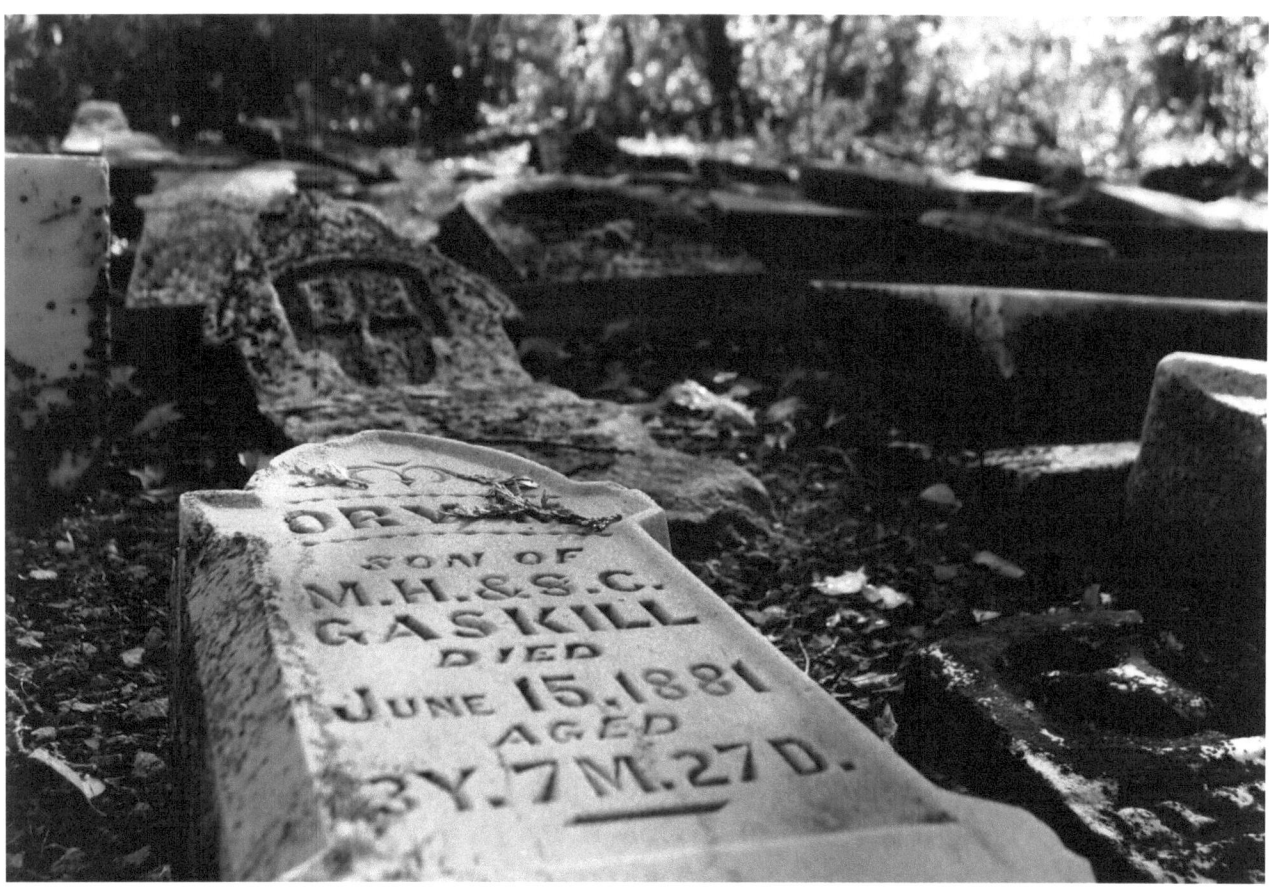

"Aged Life"
Mary McVicker

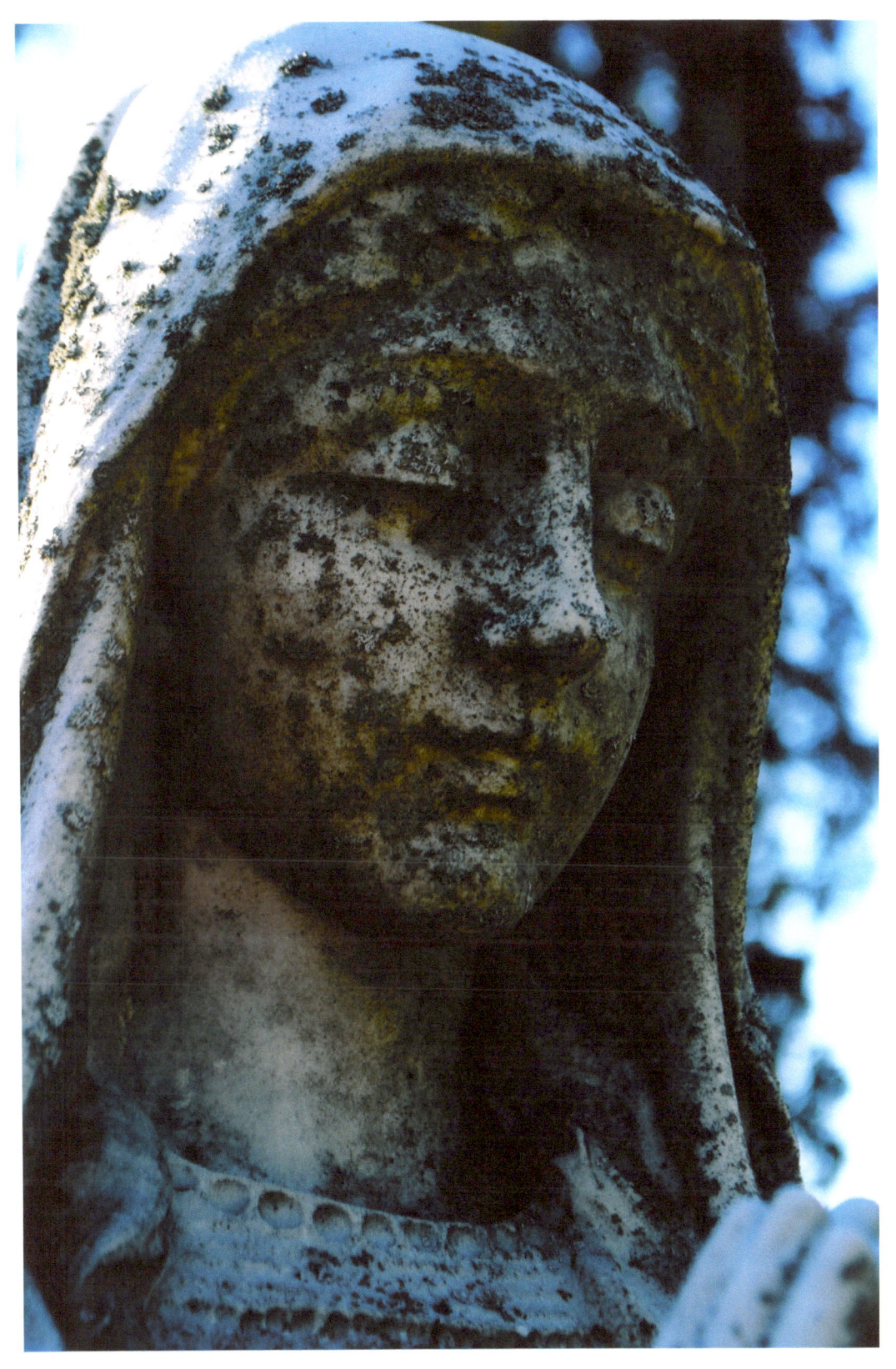

"Pure"
Mary McVicker

# Adam Gillespie

Adam Gillespie is a painter, illustrator and tattooer. He is influenced by the forbidden, and by the aspects of human nature that we are encouraged to ignore, including hedonism, greed, struggle for the alpha status, sex and violence. All of Adam's works are created in physical form.

adamgillespieartwork.com

facebook.com/beatkidsgallery

beatkidsgallery@gmail.com

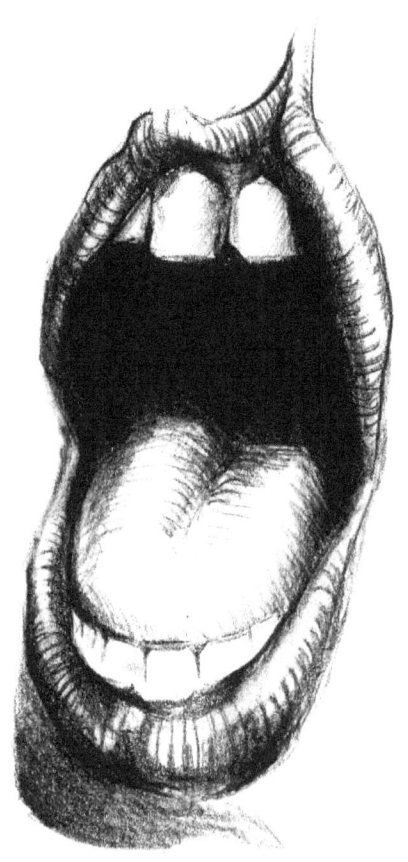

"Cleft Palate"
Adam Gillespie

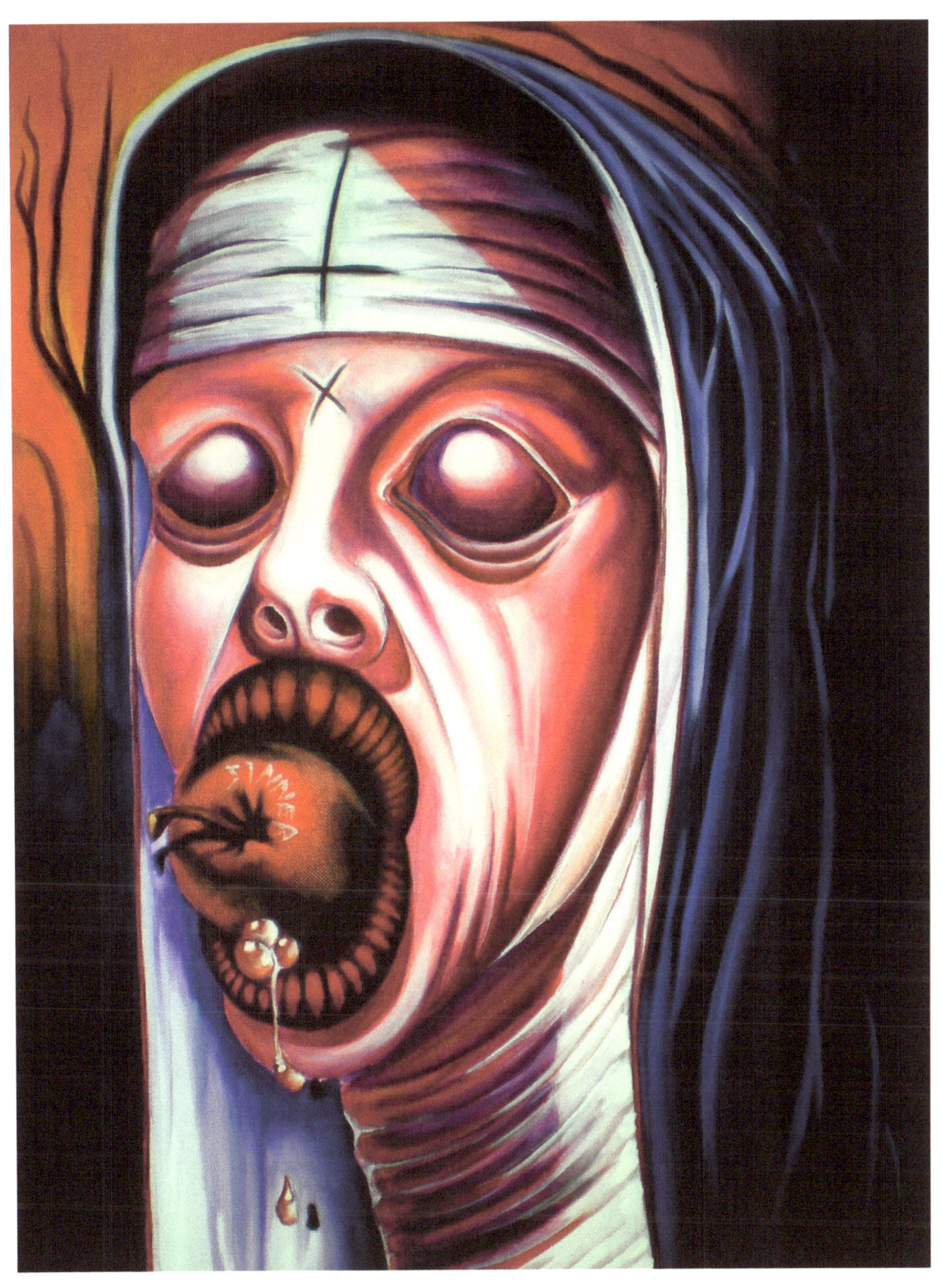

"Nuns of Romania"
Adam Gillespie

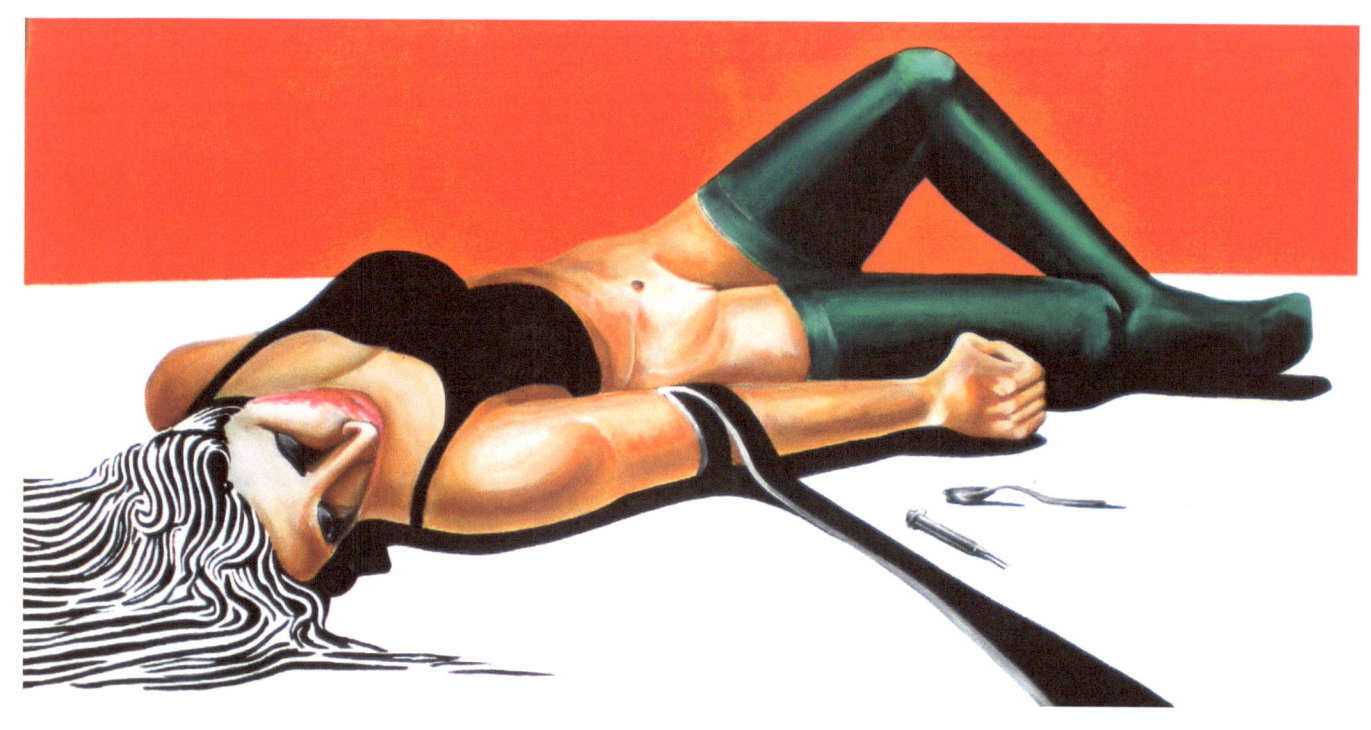

"Holiday in the Sun"
Adam Gillespie

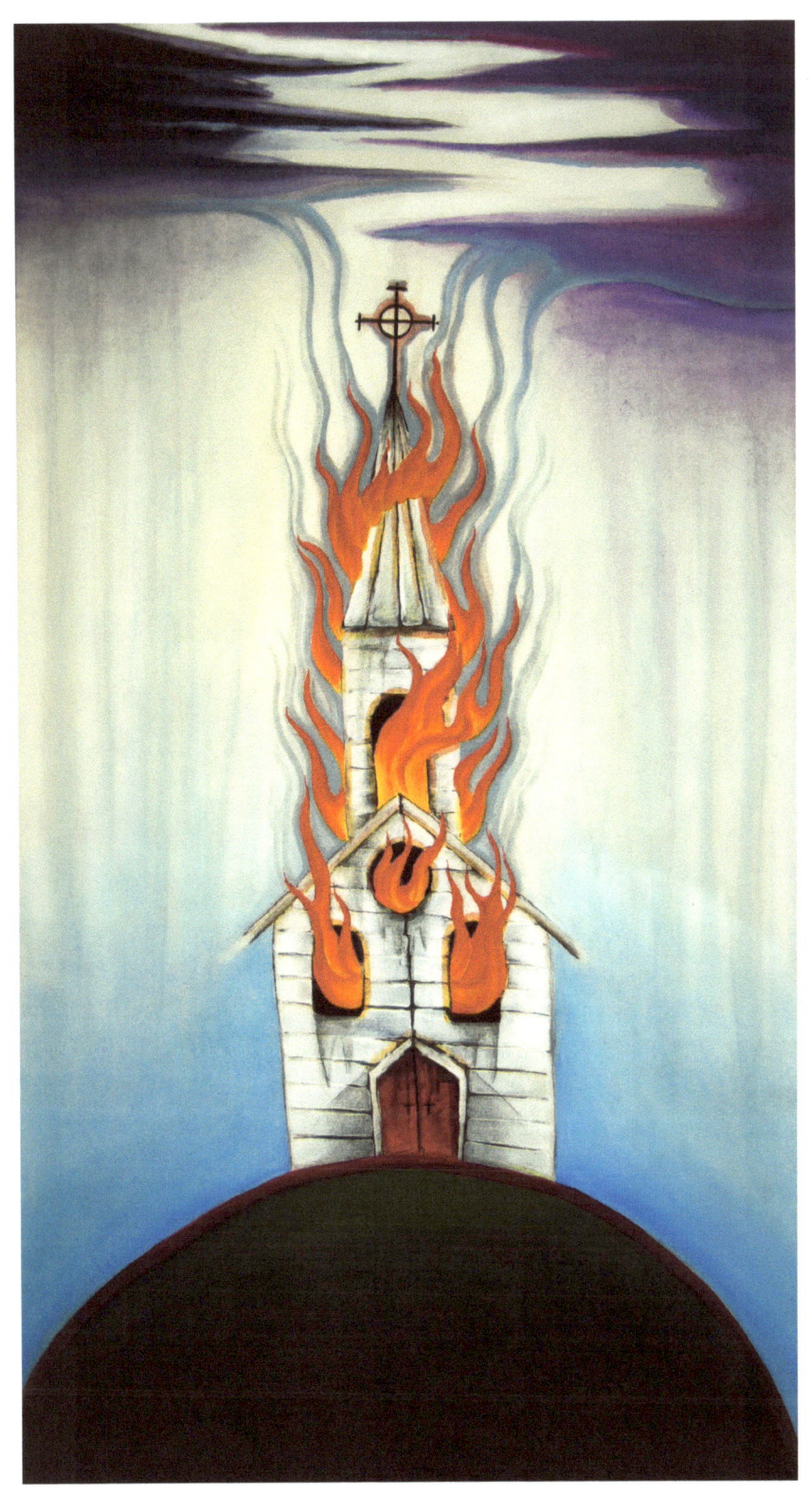

"Burning Church"
Adam Gillespie

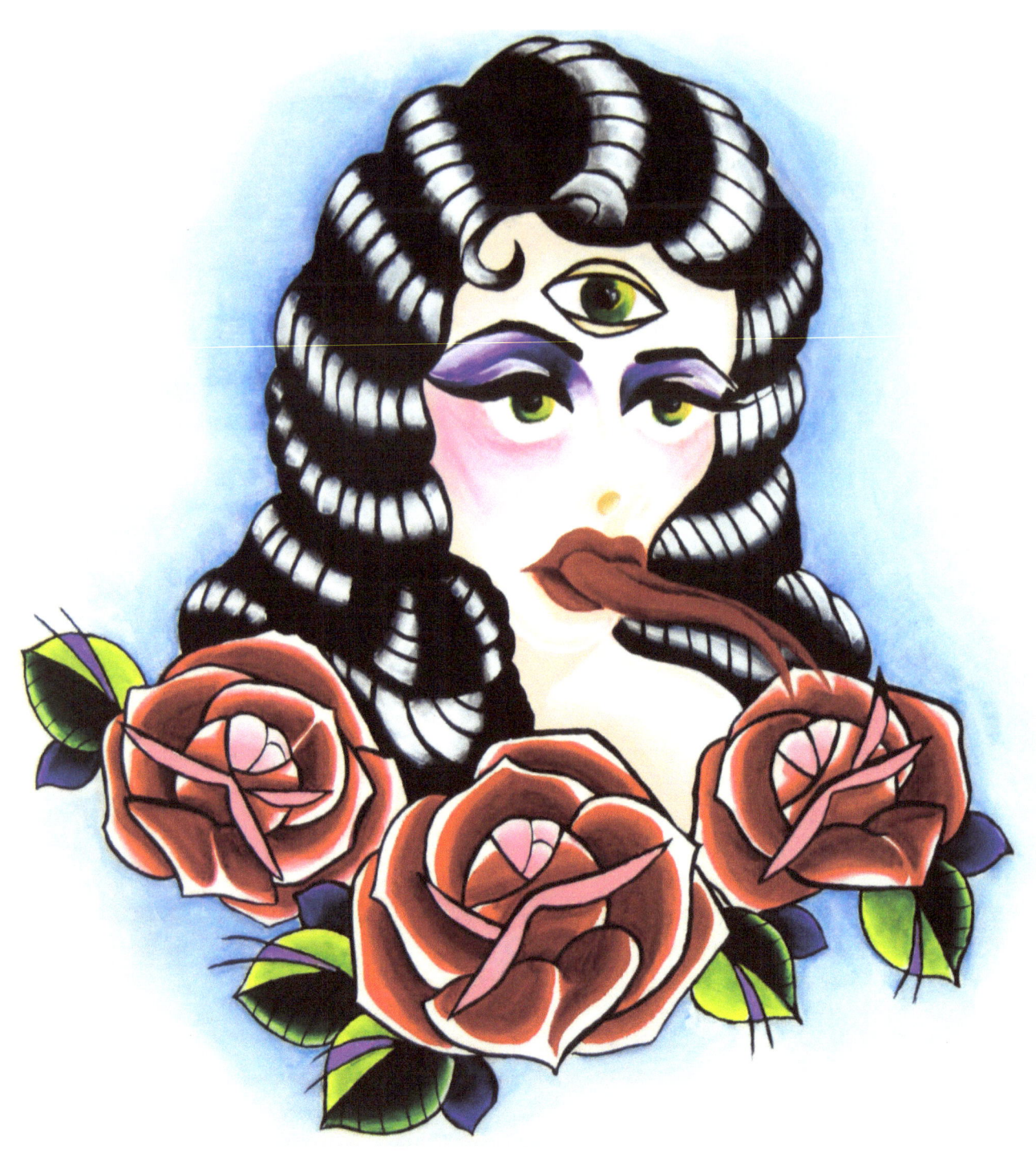

"Whore"
Adam Gillespie

# Marc Henderson

is a professional photographer living and working in Chicago IL. He is a commercial product photographer by trade but loves all types of photography, including street, landscape, portrait, and fine art. His photography hero's include Henri Cartier-Bresson and Alfred Stieglitz. His work has been displayed in shows locally as well as in Budapest.

marcdhenderson@yahoo.com
marchendersonphotography.com

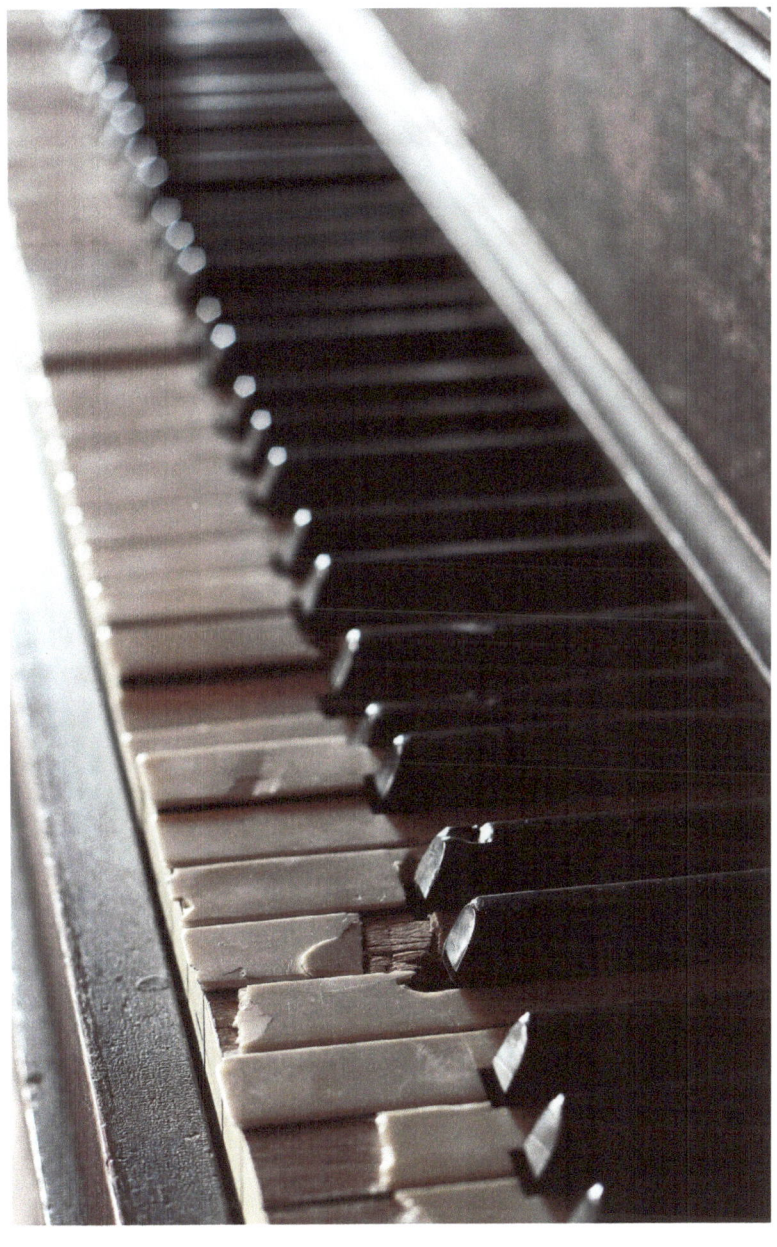

"Broken Keys"
Marc Henderson

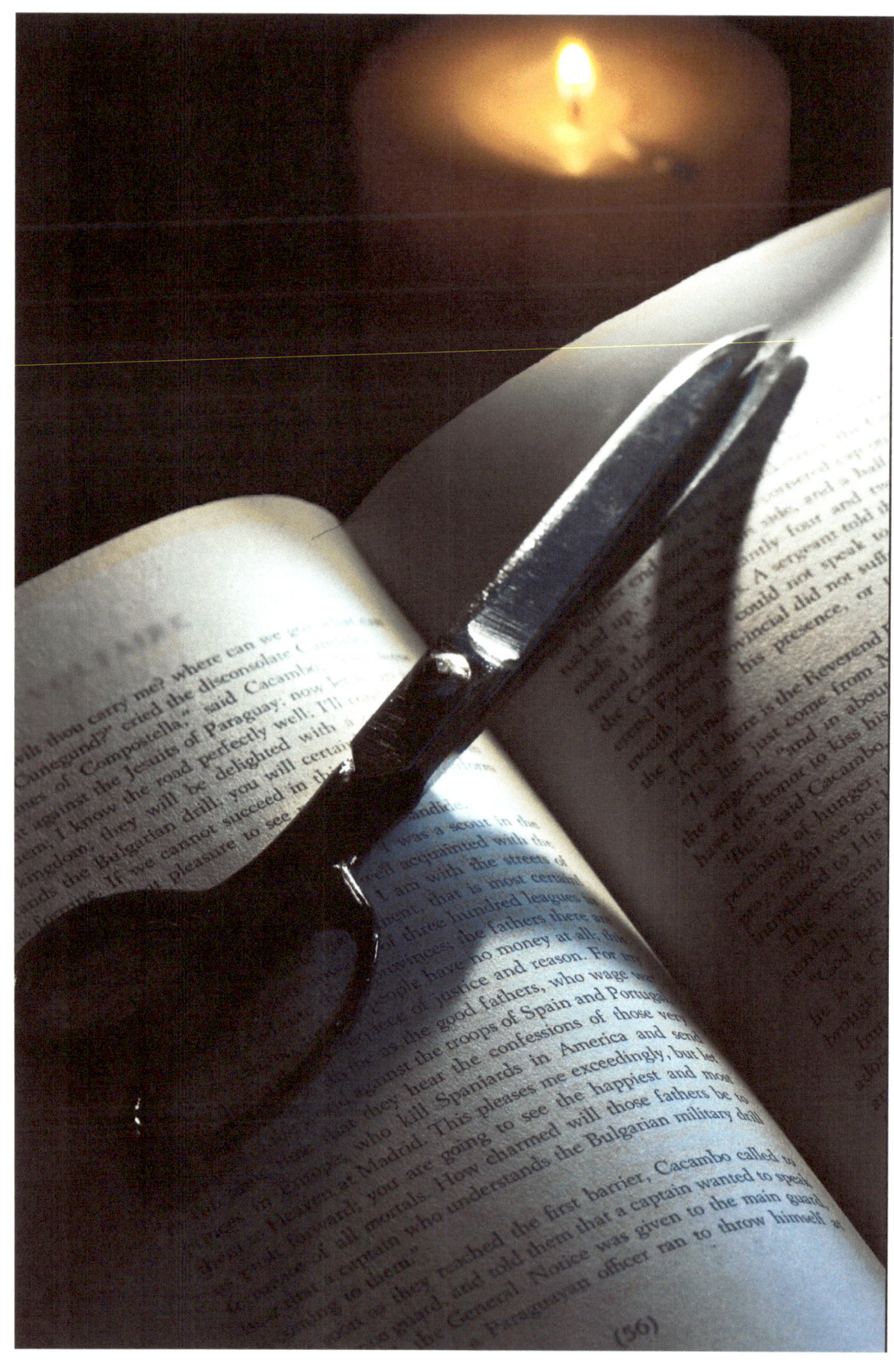

"The Book #1"
Marc Henderson

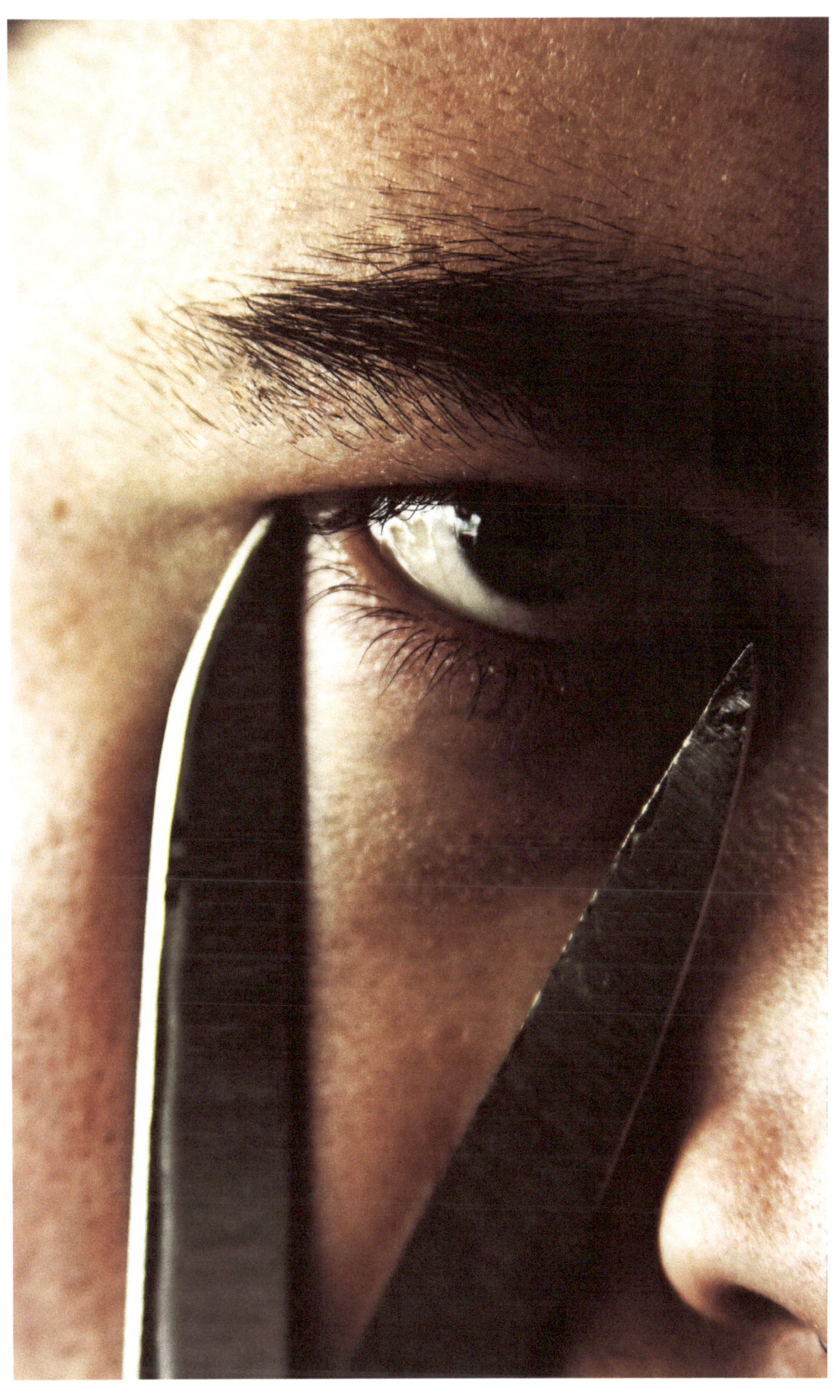

"The Book #2"
Marc Henderson

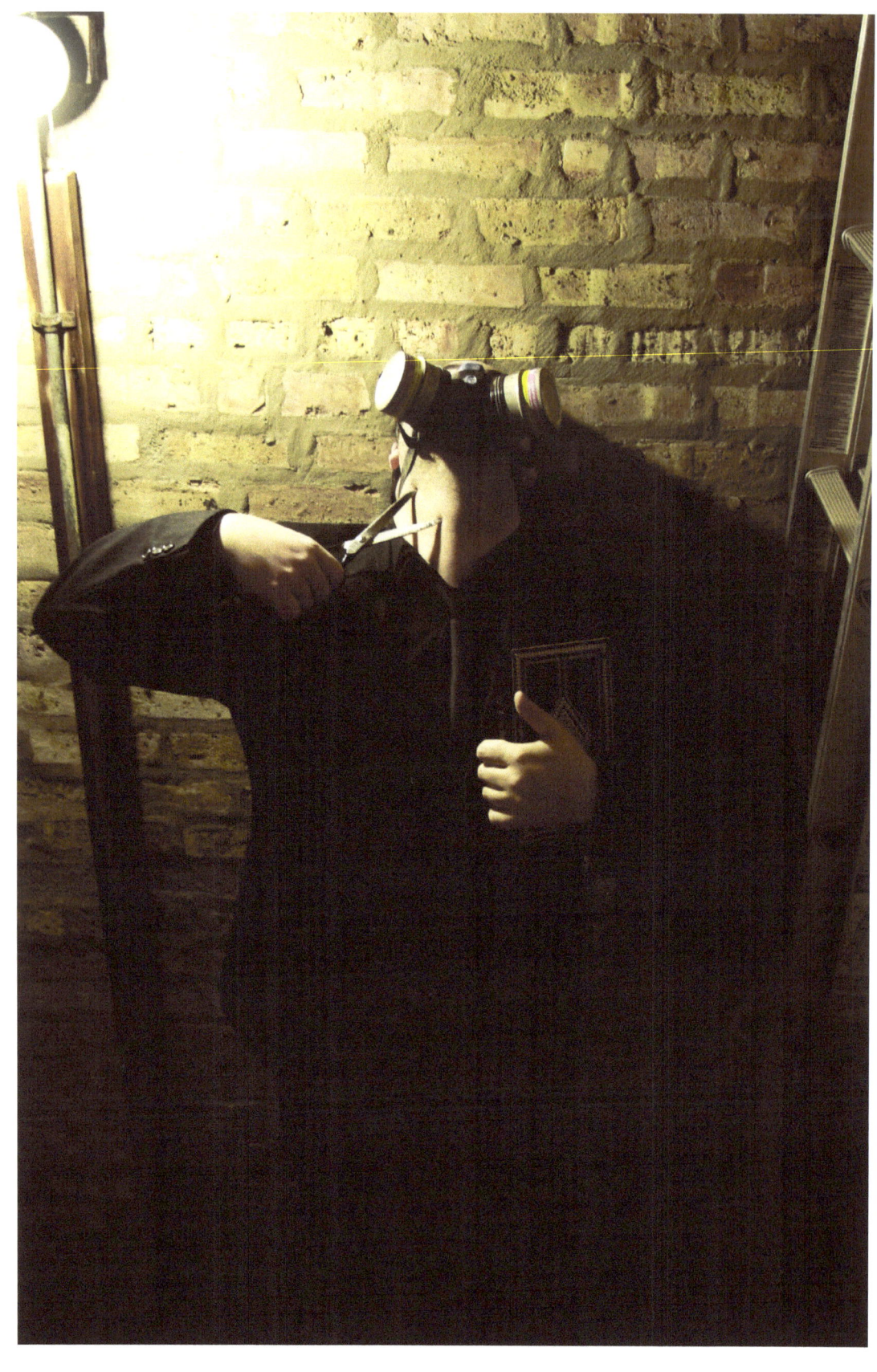

"The Book #3"
Marc Henderson

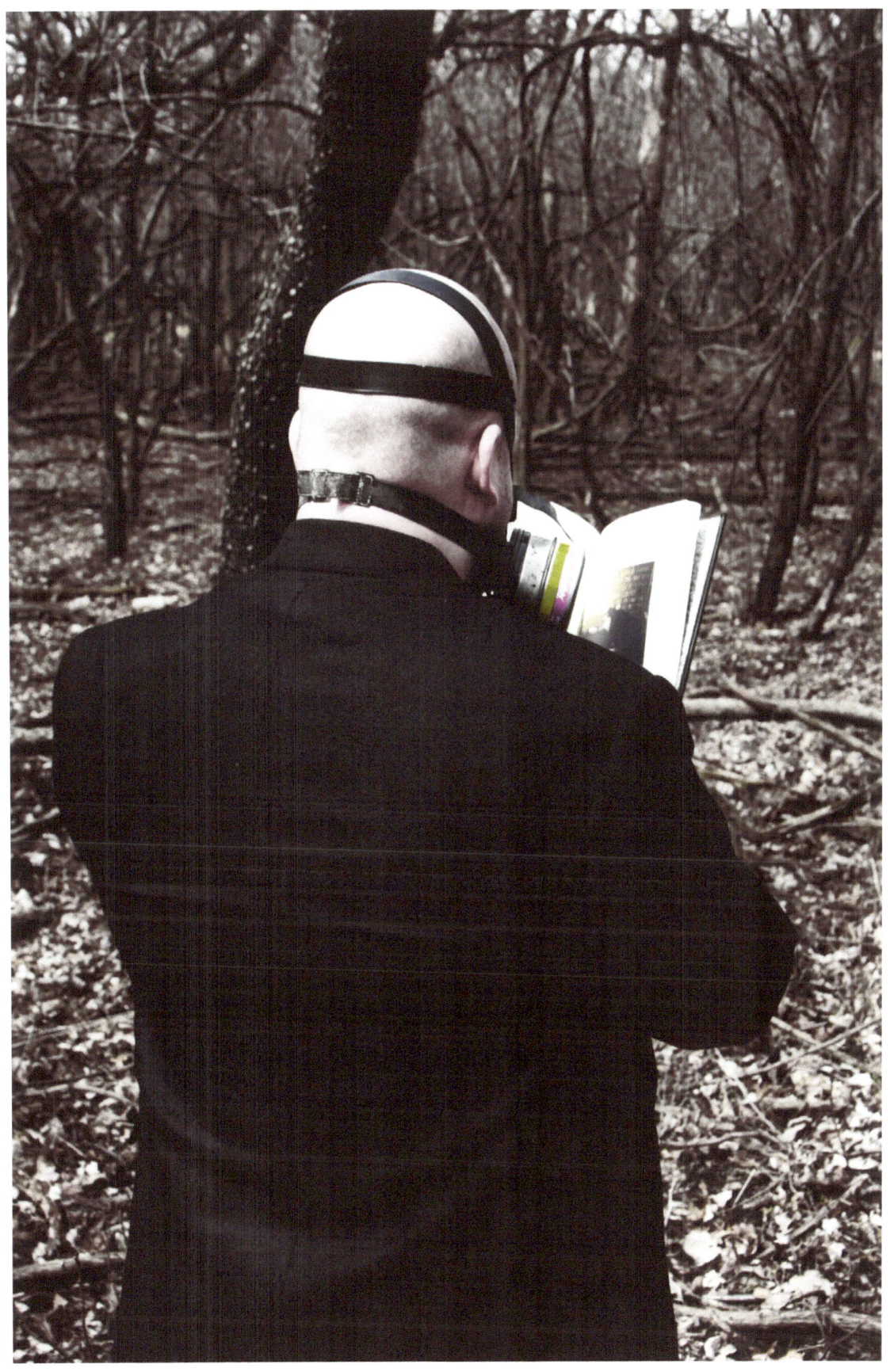

"The Book #4"
Marc Henderson

# Frederique Boulay is a talented artist and graphic designer from
Quebec, Canada.

www.frederiqueboulay.com

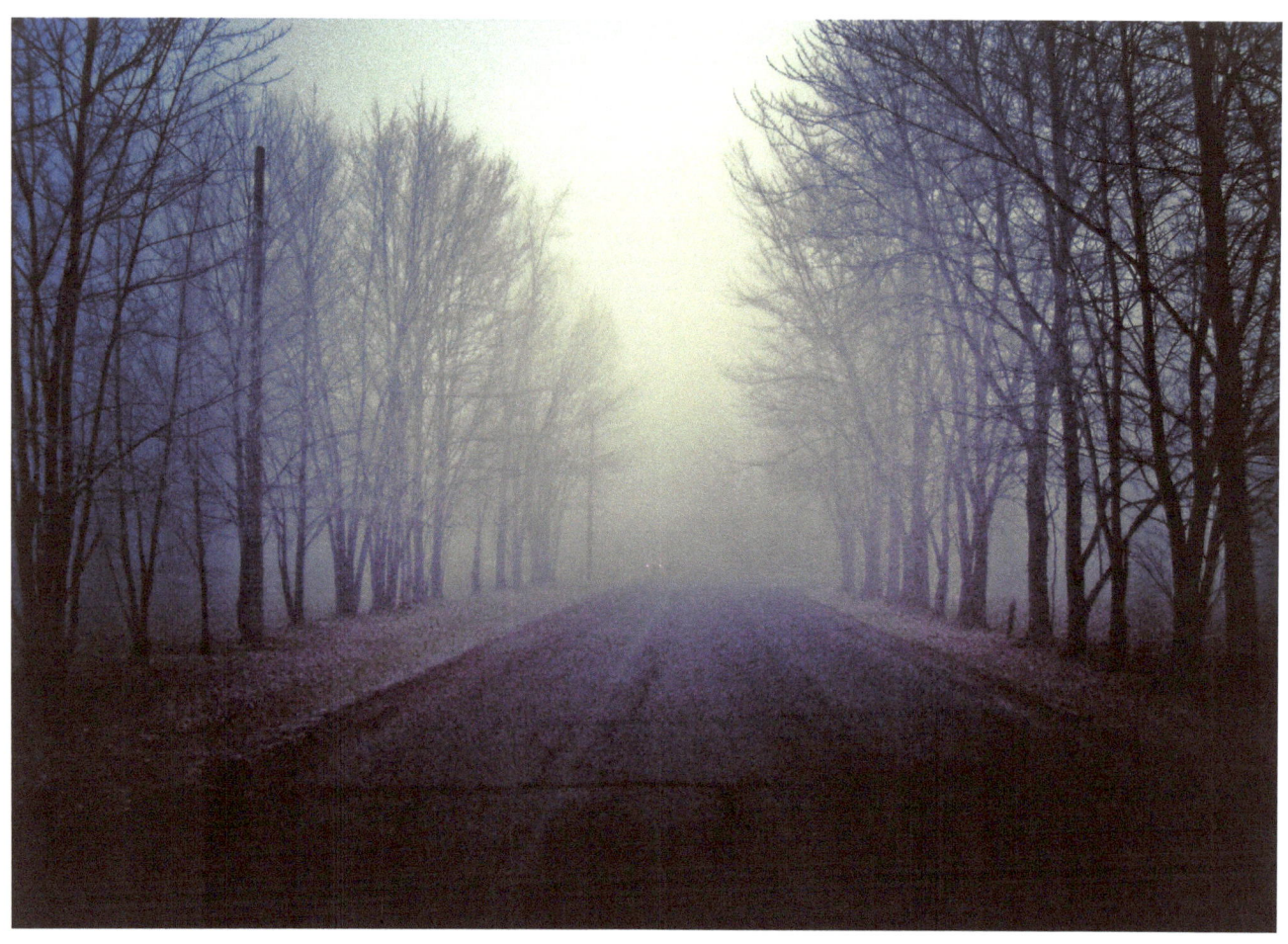

"Eerie Road"
Frederique Boulay

# Robert Treece

I use painting to bypass the limitations and delusions of my conscious experience. The Images and dreamscapes I paint are manifestations of unconscious, undifferentiated energy I am fiendishly fascinated by. The logic in my work is based on instinct. Instinct is why migrating birds don't carry roadmaps. It is easy to over think. It is hard to stop the monologue of the meaning fabricating conscious mind that never shuts up and seldom makes sense. It is a discipline to put the restriction of consciousness down like a bag of bricks and subject oneself to the dissolving, transcending, transmuting mist of wonder just below the surface of everything.

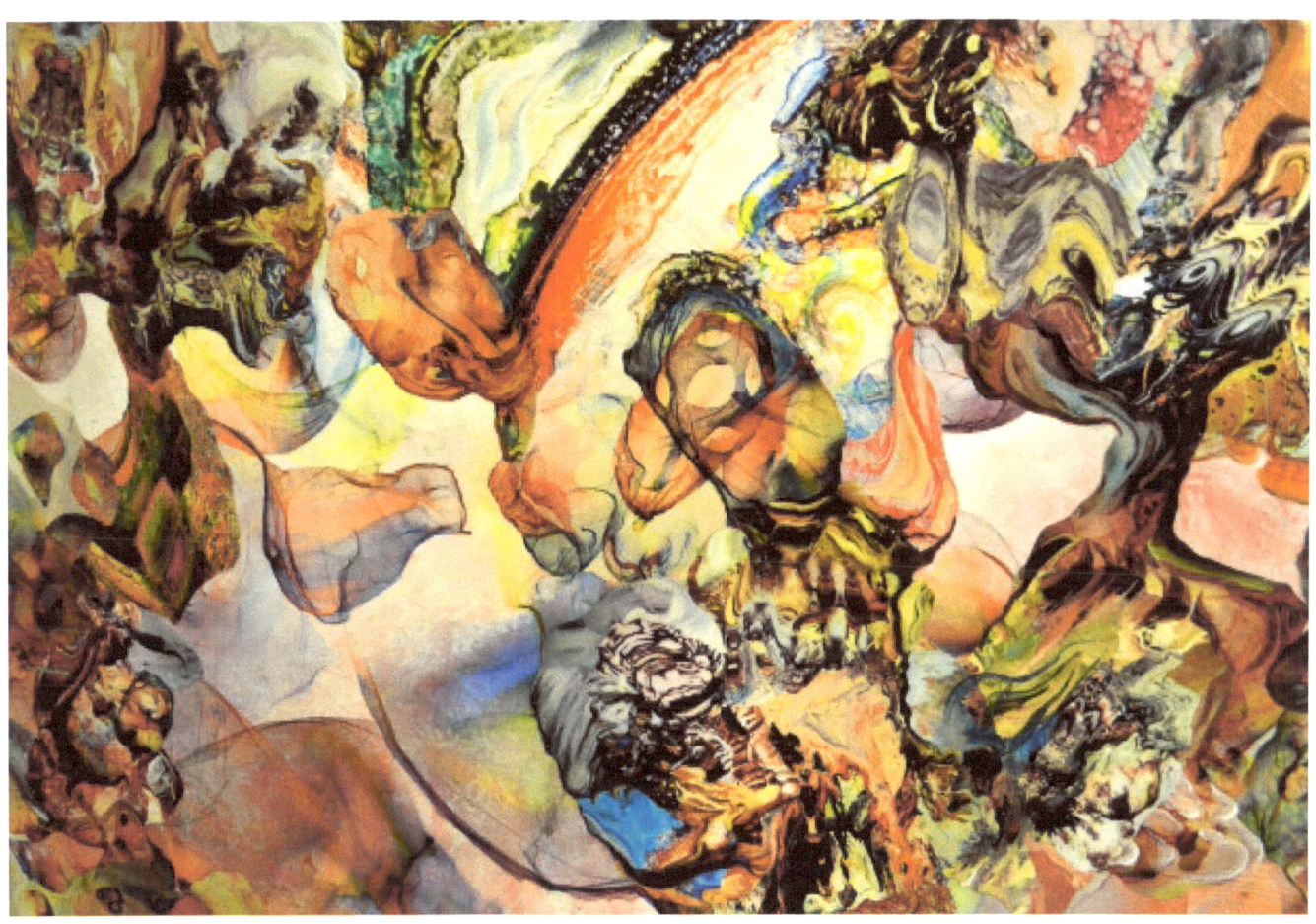

"The Bendable River"
Robert Treece

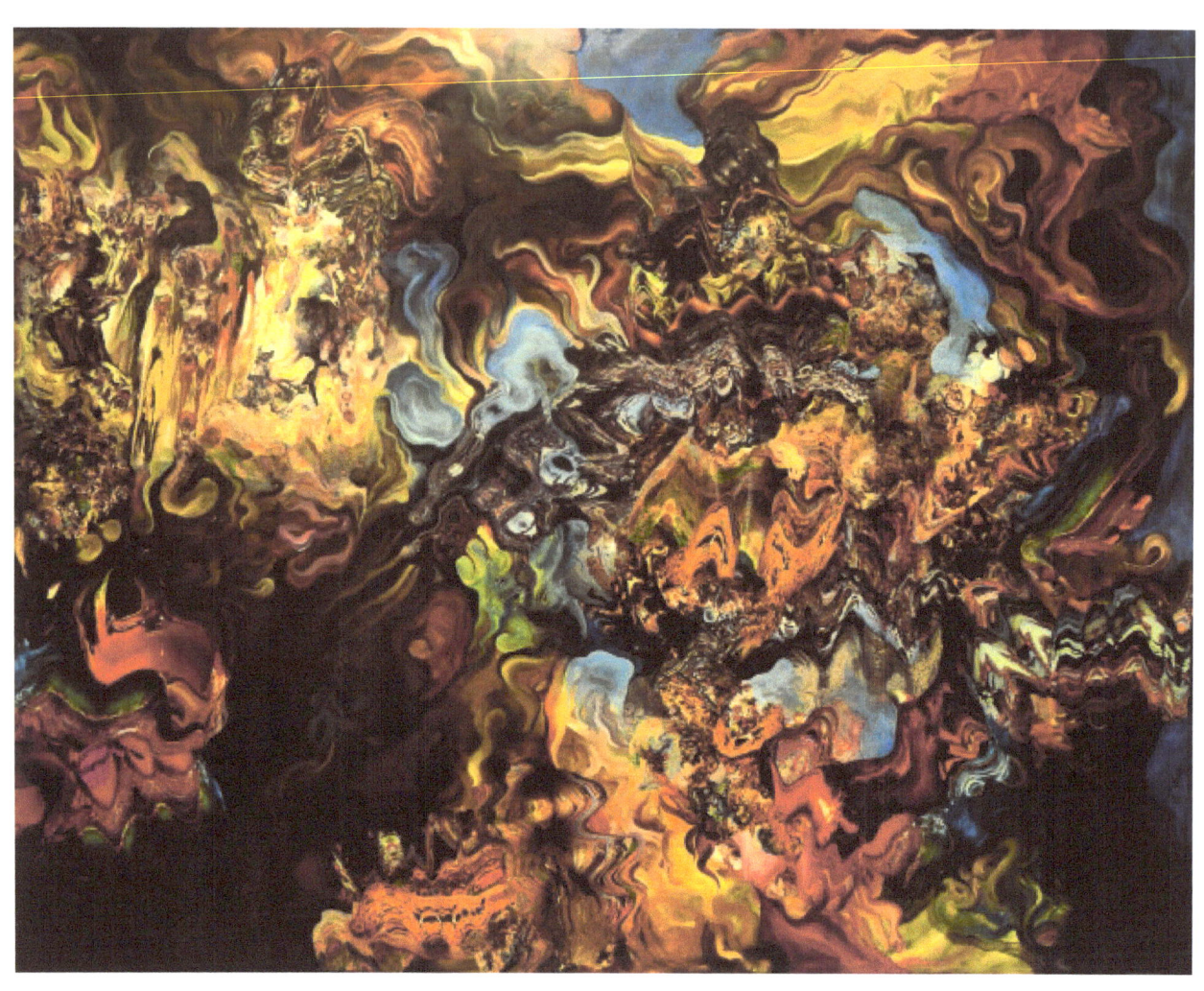

"Victory Crushed Flat by Dreary Biology"
Robert Treece

**Nick Biancardi** is currently studying Visual Communications and Graphic Arts at Purdue University Calumet in Hammond, Indiana. Nick is an amateur photographer and graphic designer who enjoys a wide array of art.

nickbiancardiportfolio.weebly.com

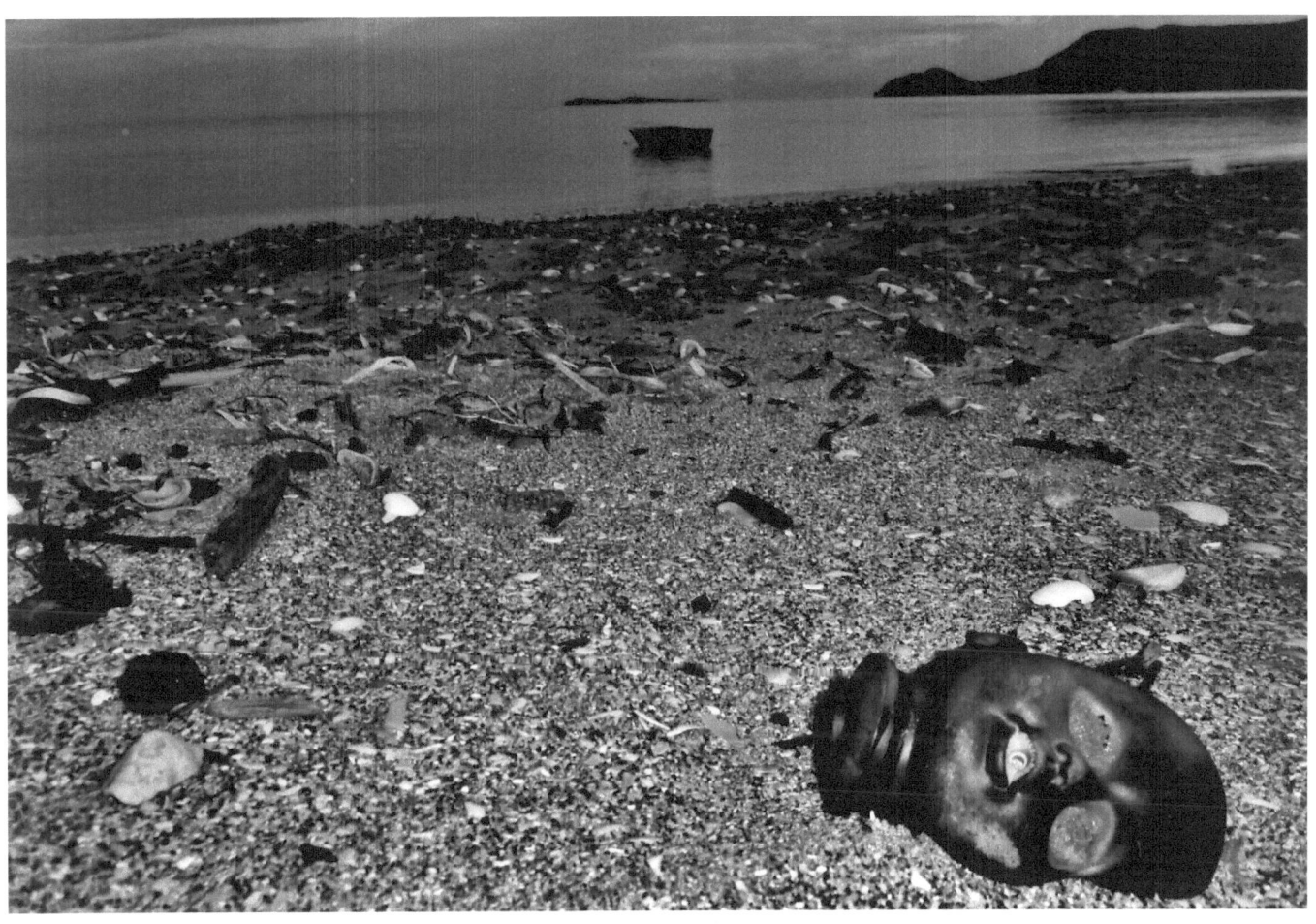

"Voodoo Head"
Nick Biancardi

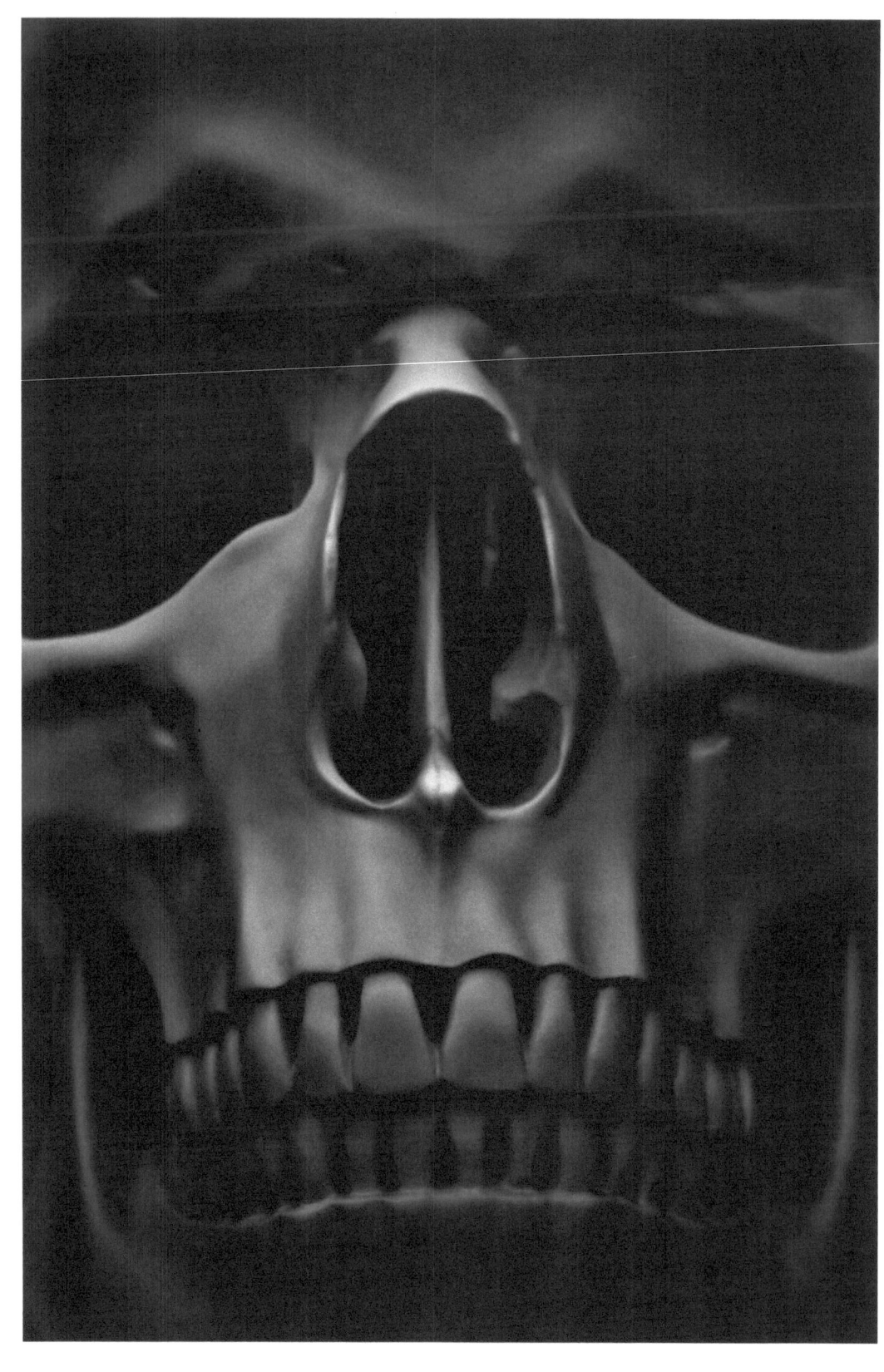

"Roof Skull"
Nick Biancardi

# Robert Willmore Artist, photographer, sculptor, fringe dweller.

"The Art must come out"...

raw4art@sbcglobal.net

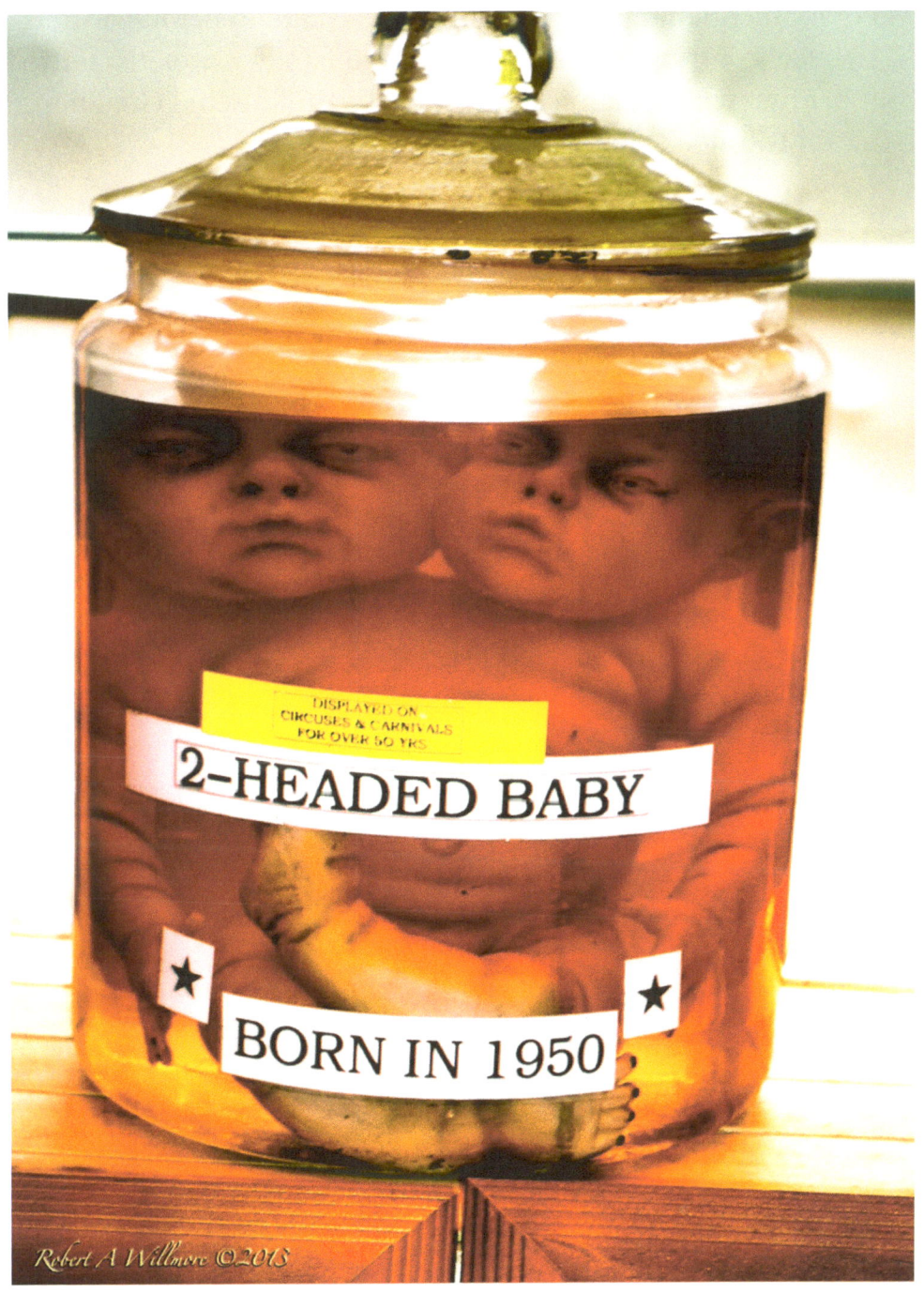

"Two Heads"
Robert Willmore

**Carol Estes** is one quirky girl with a camera. She found photography late in life, but now this girl is obsessed. Carol was born in Kansas, raised in Missouri, and moved an hour east of Chicago over 33 years ago. This background really reflects what she sees thru the lens. She loves 'moments in time', architecture, structure, birds, nature, and the amazing power of mother nature. She has come to this point in her life, with the amazing support and 'unbiased' contribution of my friends and family. Carol just started her own note cards, with her first retail location at the Mark Twain Museum Gift Shop. She is also a stock contributor on two stock photography sites.

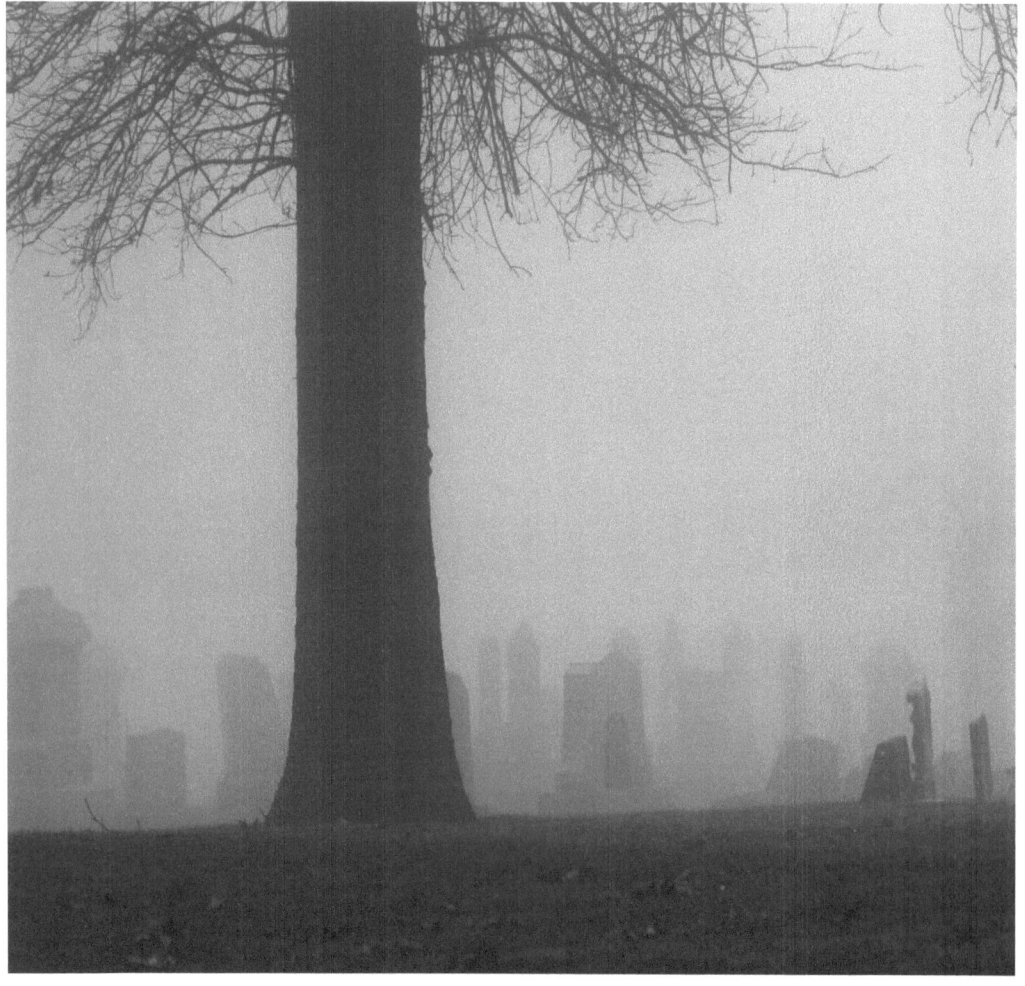

"Peace in Eternity"
Carol Estes

# Alma Peralta

Alma's work goes from fantasy to the surrealism in a way that reflects her feelings and emotions. Through her art she tells a story, sometimes from dreams and others from her own life experiences. With this silent medium she speaks loudly and gives us in each canvas a unique expression of herself. Born in Vega Baja, Puerto Rico, Alma was a shy little who had always loved colors and paint. By the age of 4 she began drawing images inspired by her dreams. In 1989 Alma immigrated to the United States where in 1991 she graduated Hoboken High School. Soon after she married Hector Luis Peralta and had two daughters. 2004 she joined an art program at Bridgeway in Elizabeth New Jersey, where she discovered her talent for the Arts.

In 2006, Alma registered "part-time" for art classes at Hudson County Community College in hopes to pursue a career in fine arts. Since then Alma has been painting passionately towards her goals of becoming a successful artist. She has done many exhibits around New York and New Jersey and also curated many others. Currently, she is an appointed member of the Union City Artist Collective and her work can be seen at the Union City Art Museum where it is permanently displayed.

artleejay@gmail.com

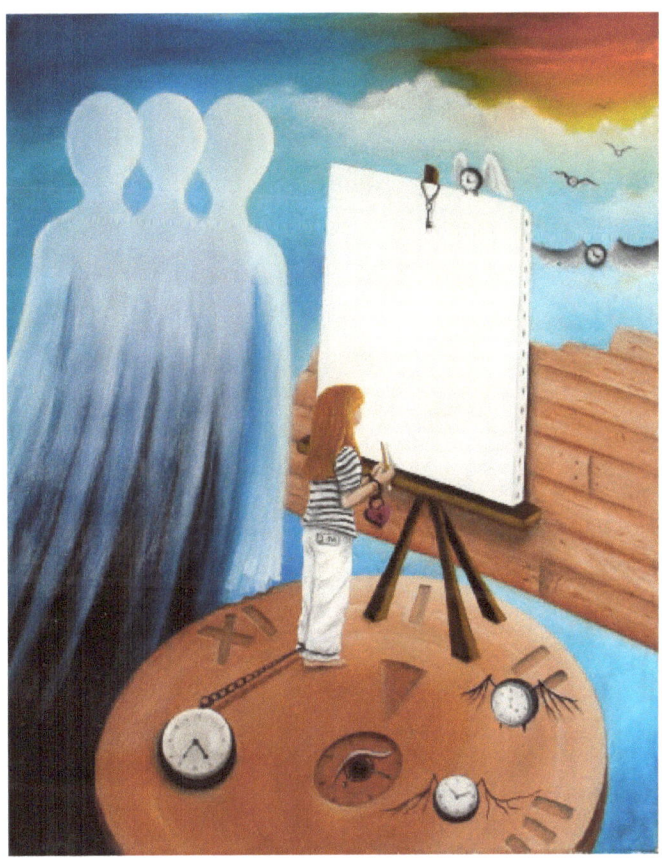

"In Due Time"
Alma Peralta

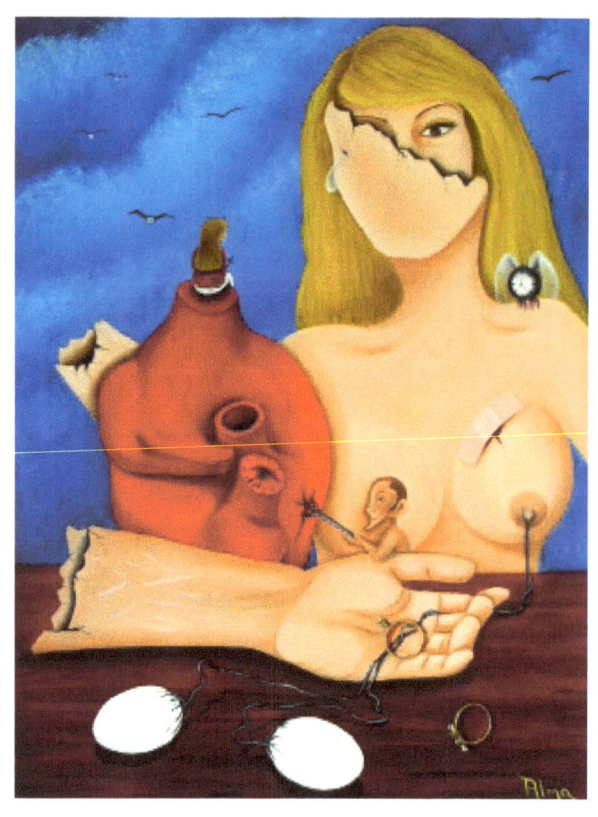

"My Divorce"
Alma Peralta

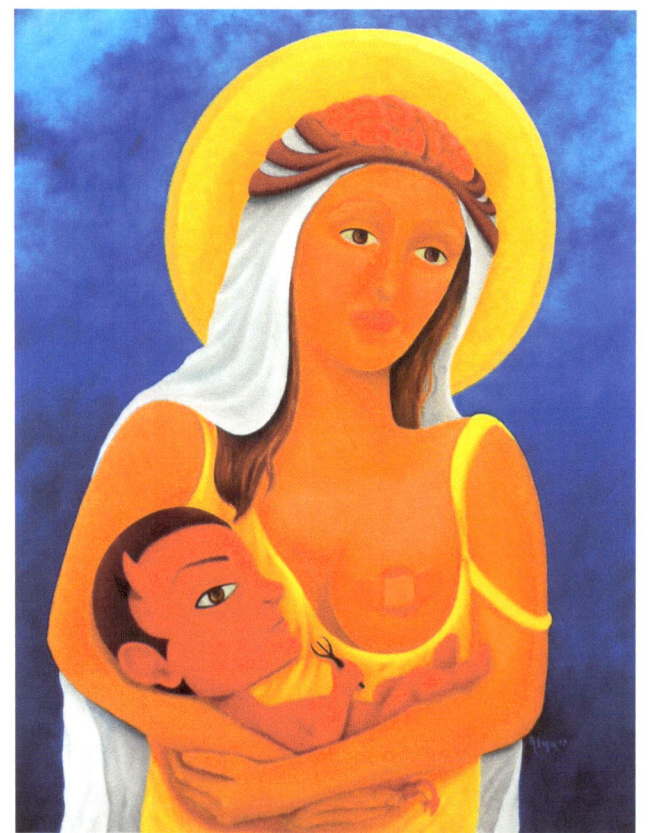

"Me and My Little Devil"
Alma Peralta

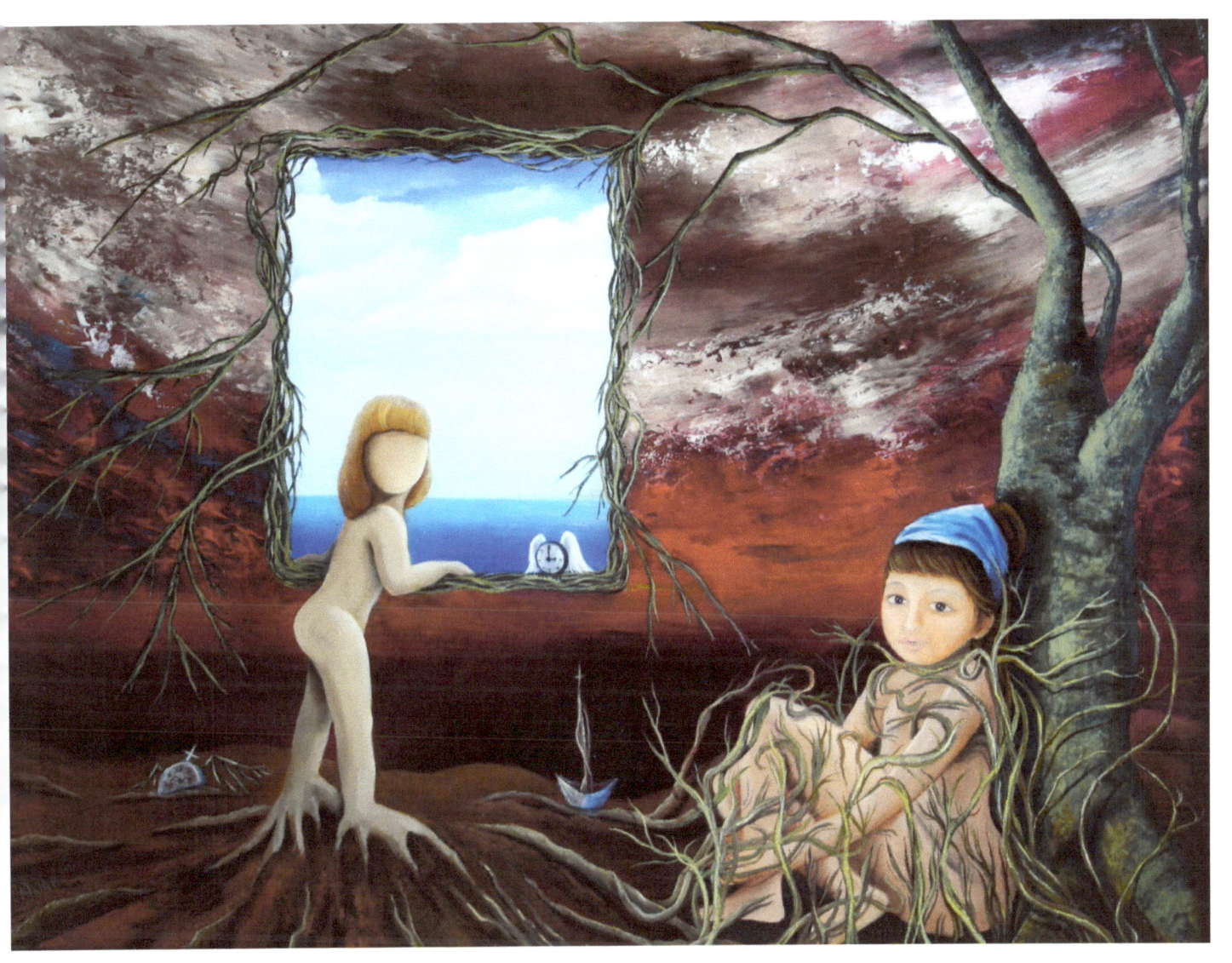

"The Illusion of Freedom"
Alma Peralta

# Lora Mercado

finds beauty and fascination in historic cemeteries. Her photography depicts how she is drawn to the nostalgia of the past. With each photo she takes, Lora strives to evoke feelings of wonder, as to who the graves belonged to and how did they live and die. There are so many stories buried under the ornate graves of long ago.

Along with photography, Lora Mercado finds enjoyment in painting, collage, and graphic design. She is also the founder and editor of Macabre Art Magazine.

loramercadophotography.com
loramercadophotography@gmail.com

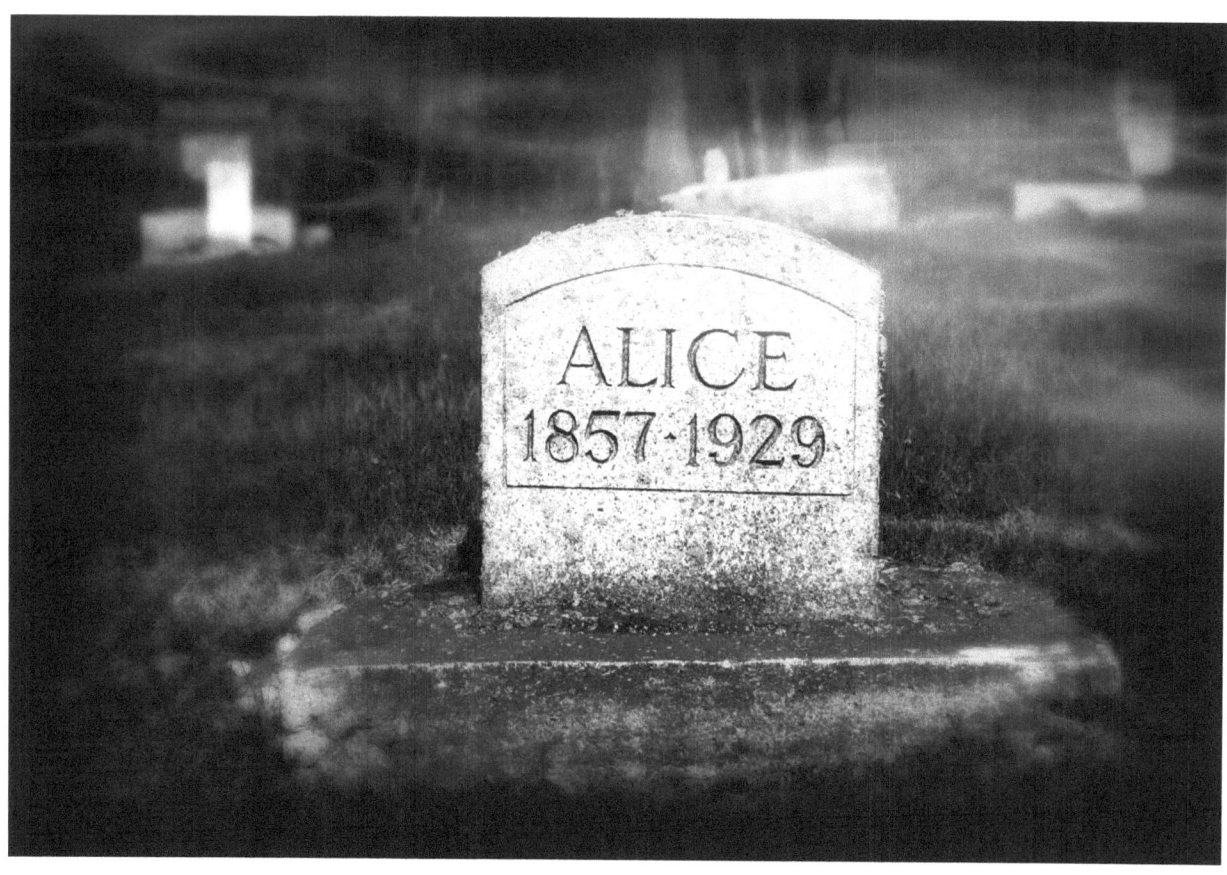

"Go Ask Alice"
Lora Mercado

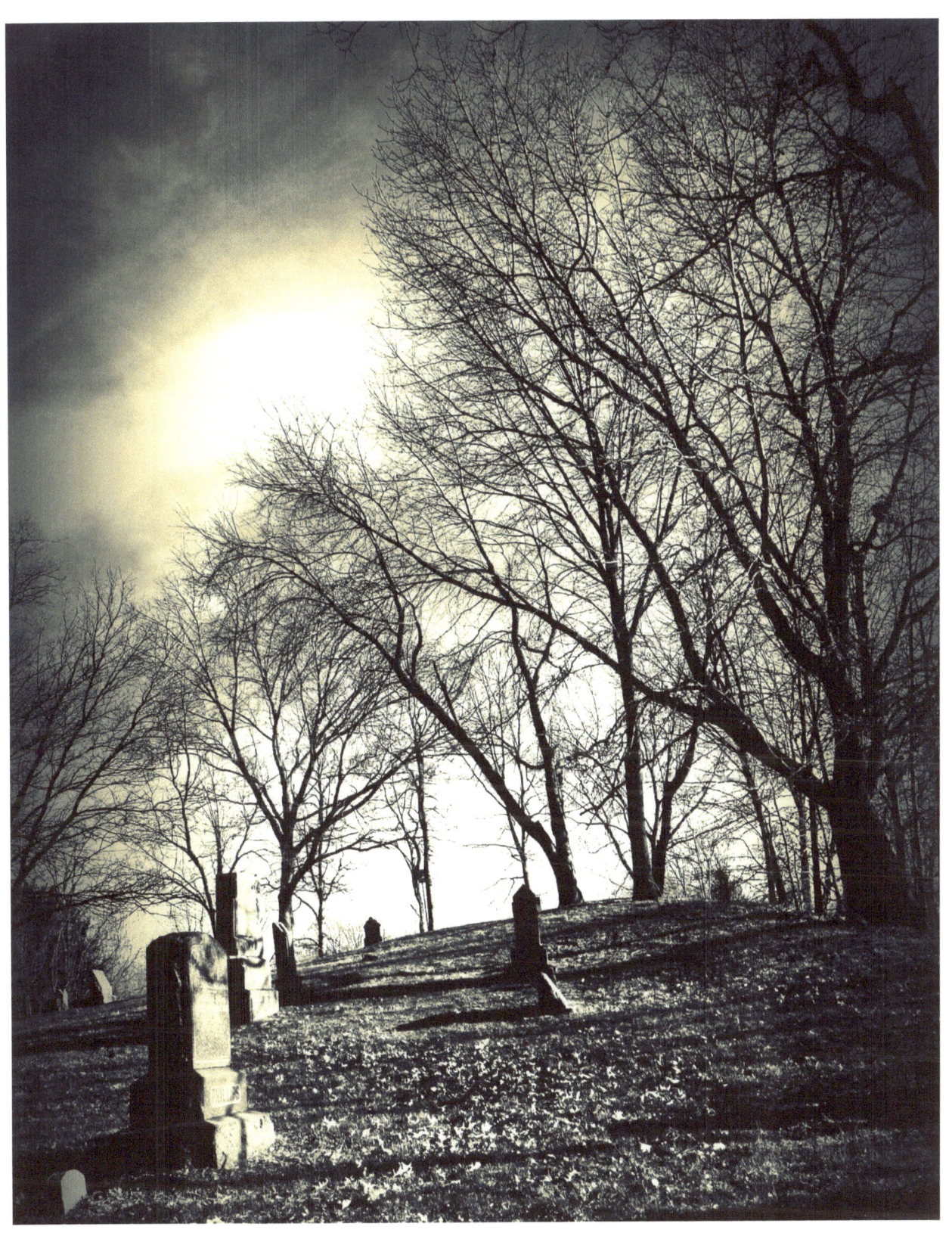

"A Grave Situation"
Lora Mercado

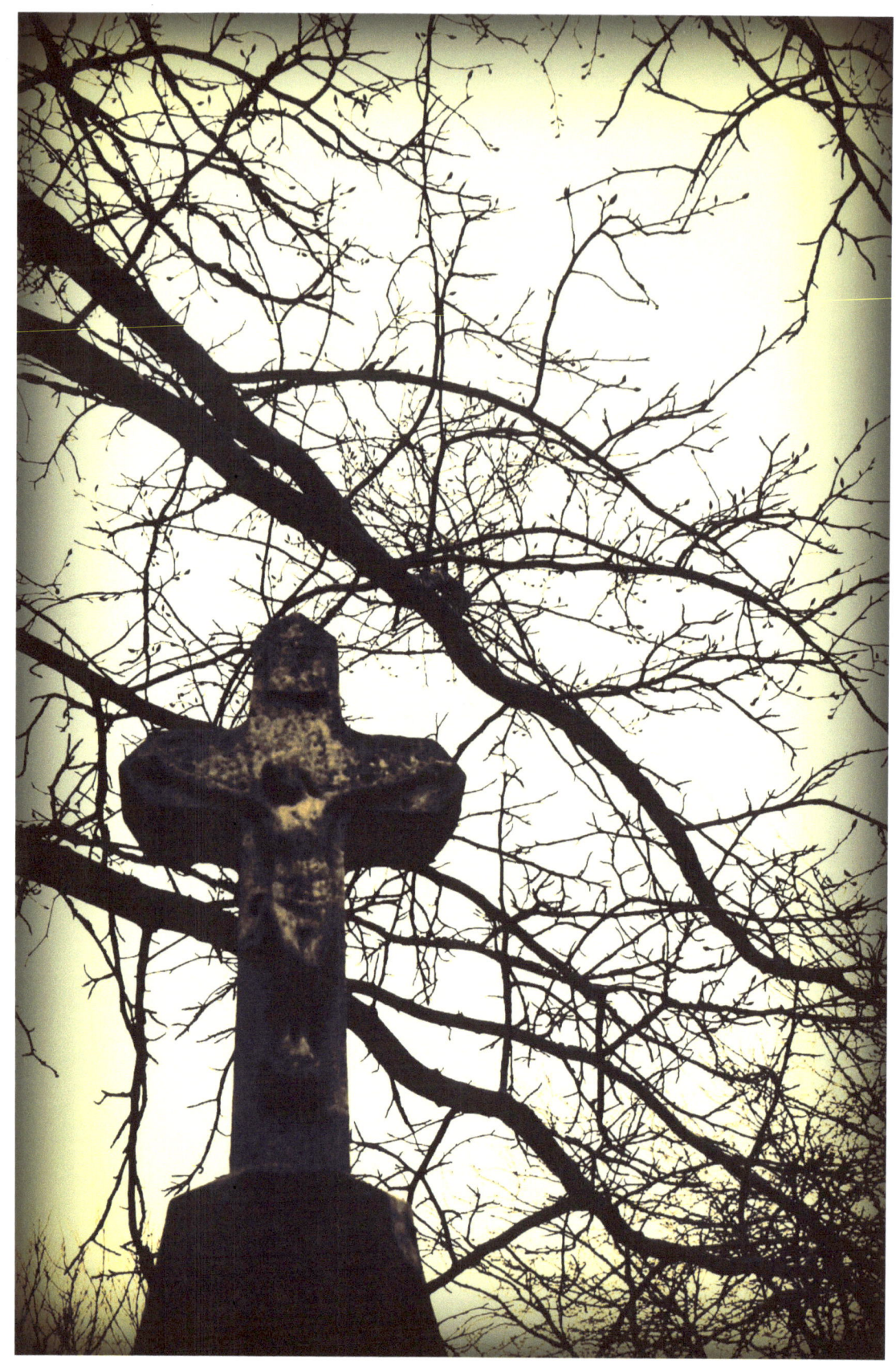

"Cross in the Trees"
Lora Mercado

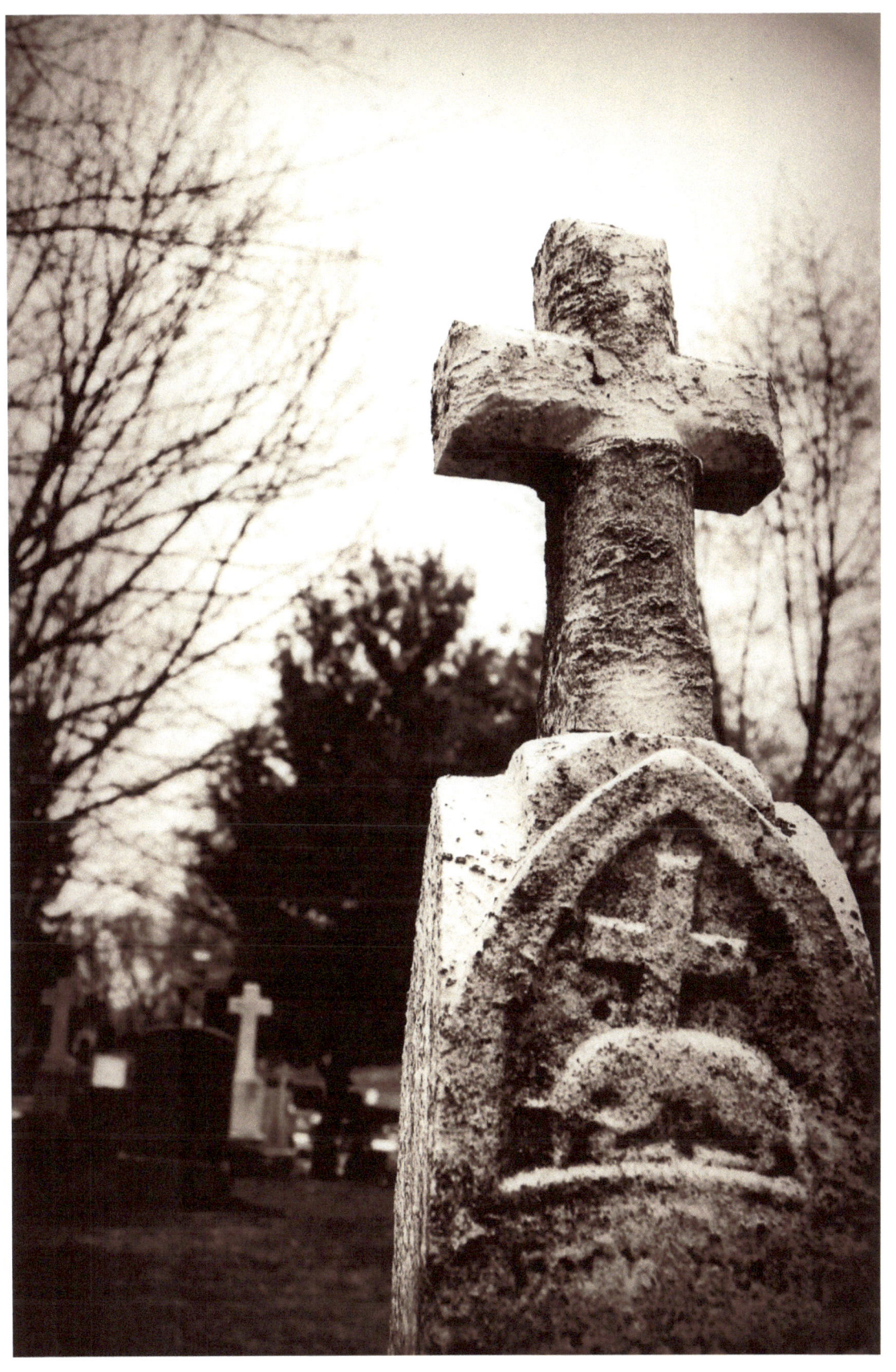

"Forgotten"
Lora Mercado

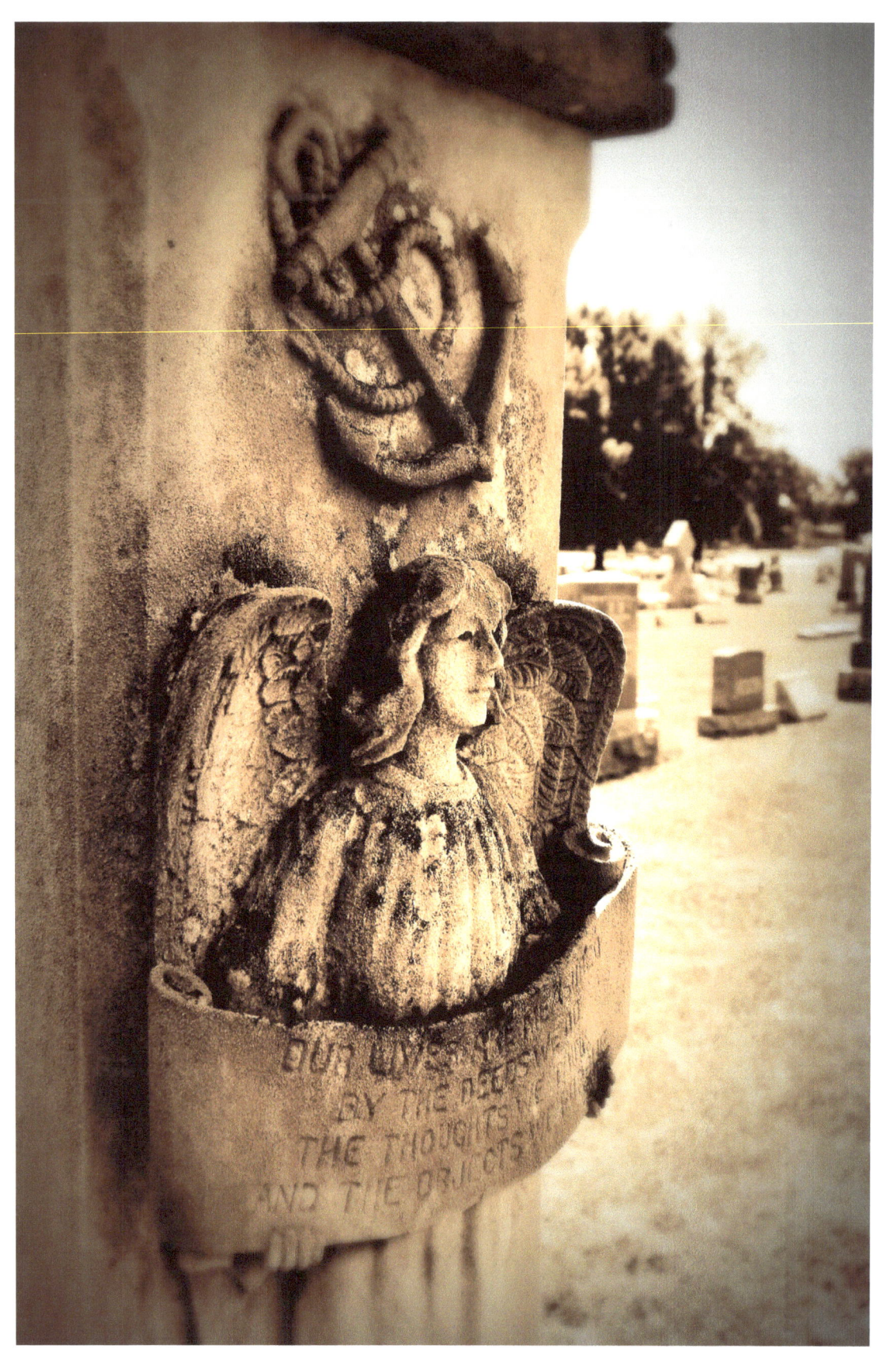

"A Sailor's Memory"
Lora Mercado

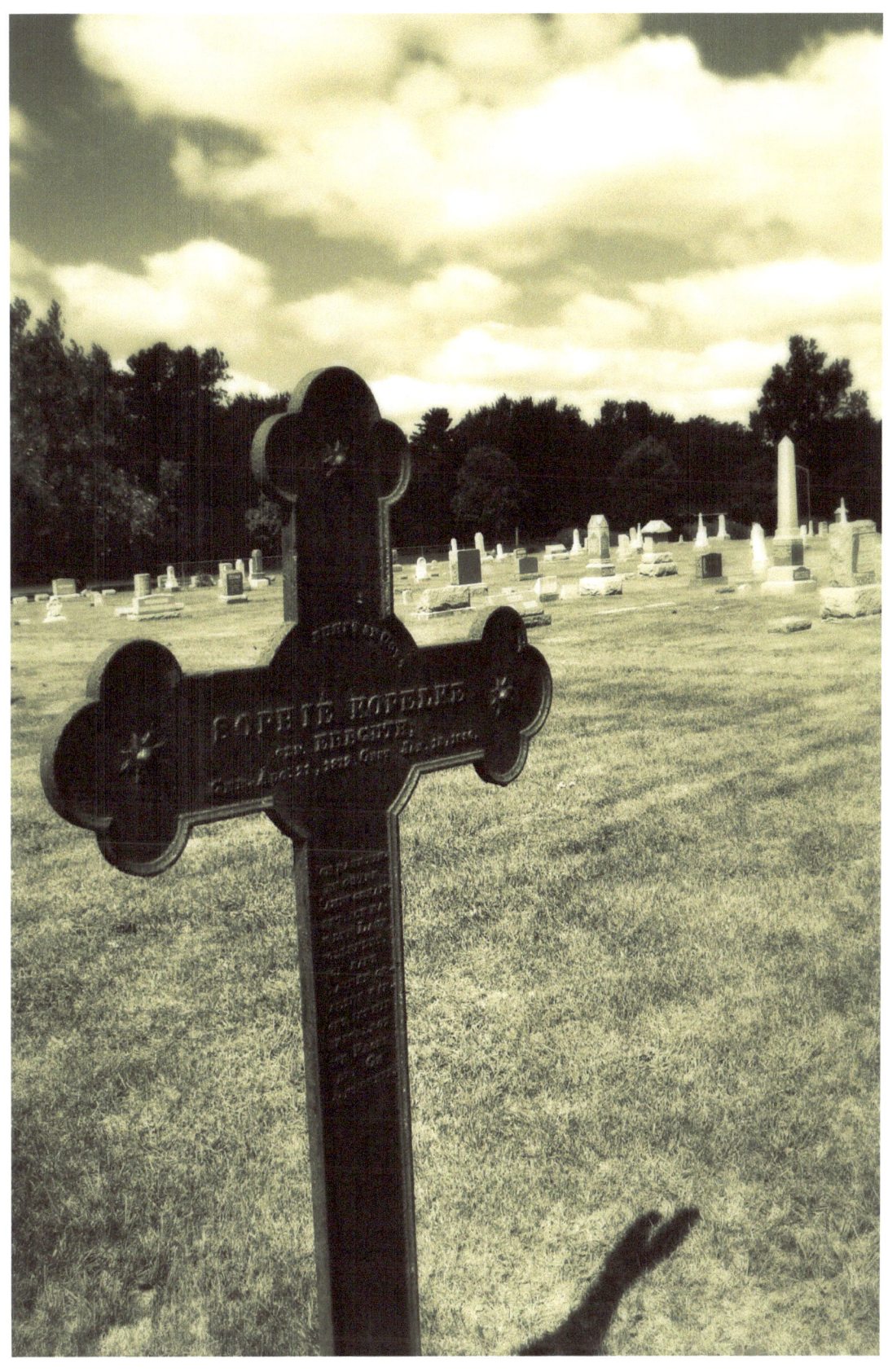

"In Memory"
Lora Mercado

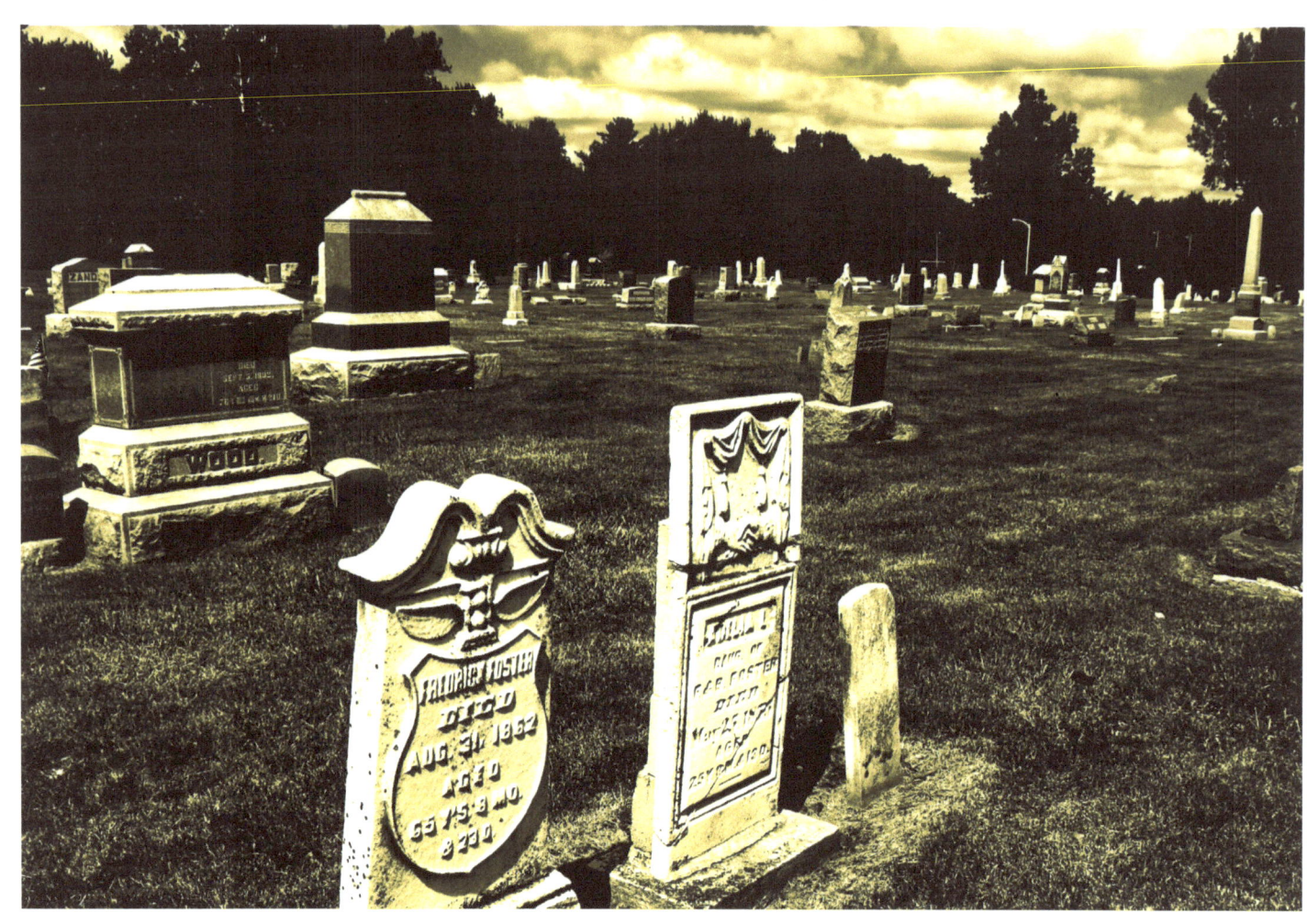

"Long Gone"
Lora Mercado

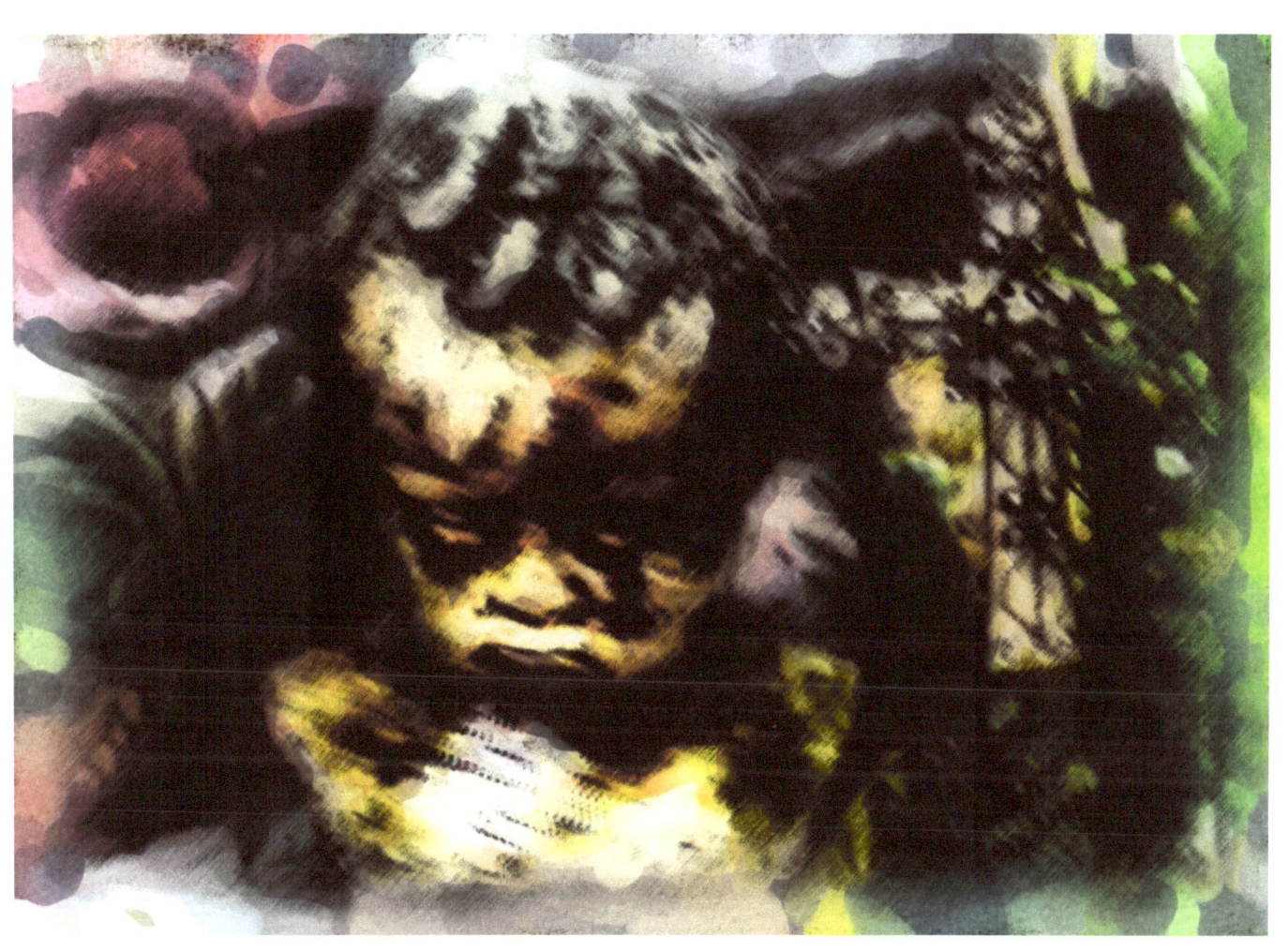

"Scary Baby"
Lora Mercado

# Dennis McCabe

is a versatile and strong conceptual thinker with exceptional sketching and writing skills with the ability to think creatively in response to diverse demands and projects with a background in storyboarding, sequential art, concept art, graphic novels, cartoons, product illustration, giftware design, social expressions, children's storybooks, humorous and non-humorous illustration, editorial and political caricature.

Dennis is an 11-year veteran caricaturist, delighting thousands of subjects at such venues as regional custom/classic car shows, cruise-ins, fairs and festivals, mall special events, country club events, wedding receptions, birthday parties, graduation parties, business events, sales meetings, Christmas parties, summer picnics, bar mitzvahs, community festivals, bars 'n taverns, charity events, political events and has drawn guests at the Cleveland Zoo, at a Six Flags amusement park and at the NFL Hall of Fame induction parties, and was resident caricaturist at Canal Park, home field of the Cleveland Indians AA farm baseball team.

dpatrickmccabe@yahoo.com

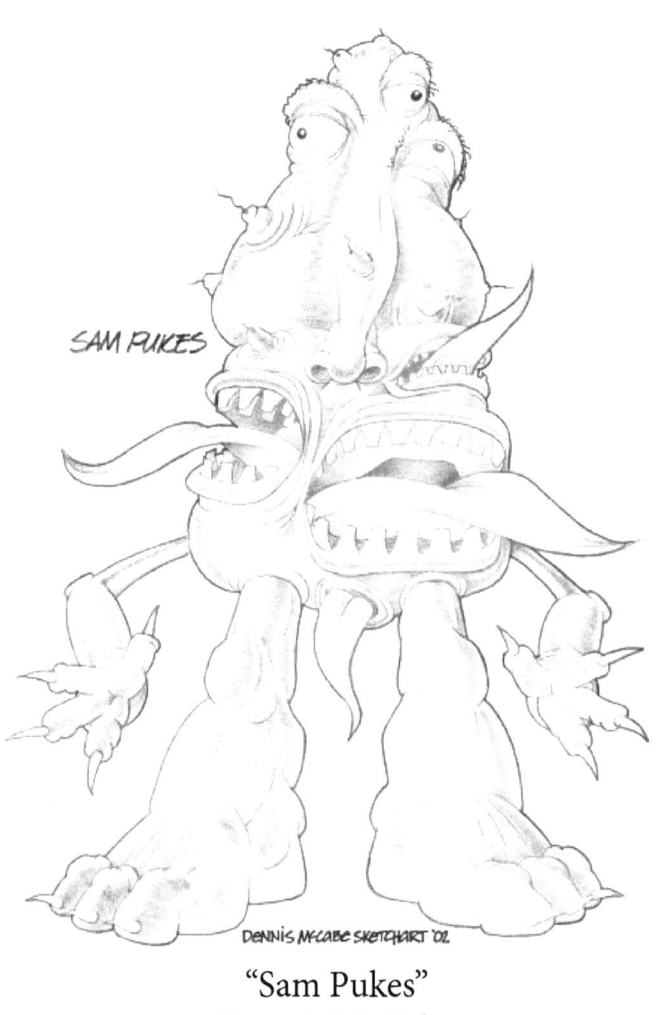

"Sam Pukes"
Dennis McCabe

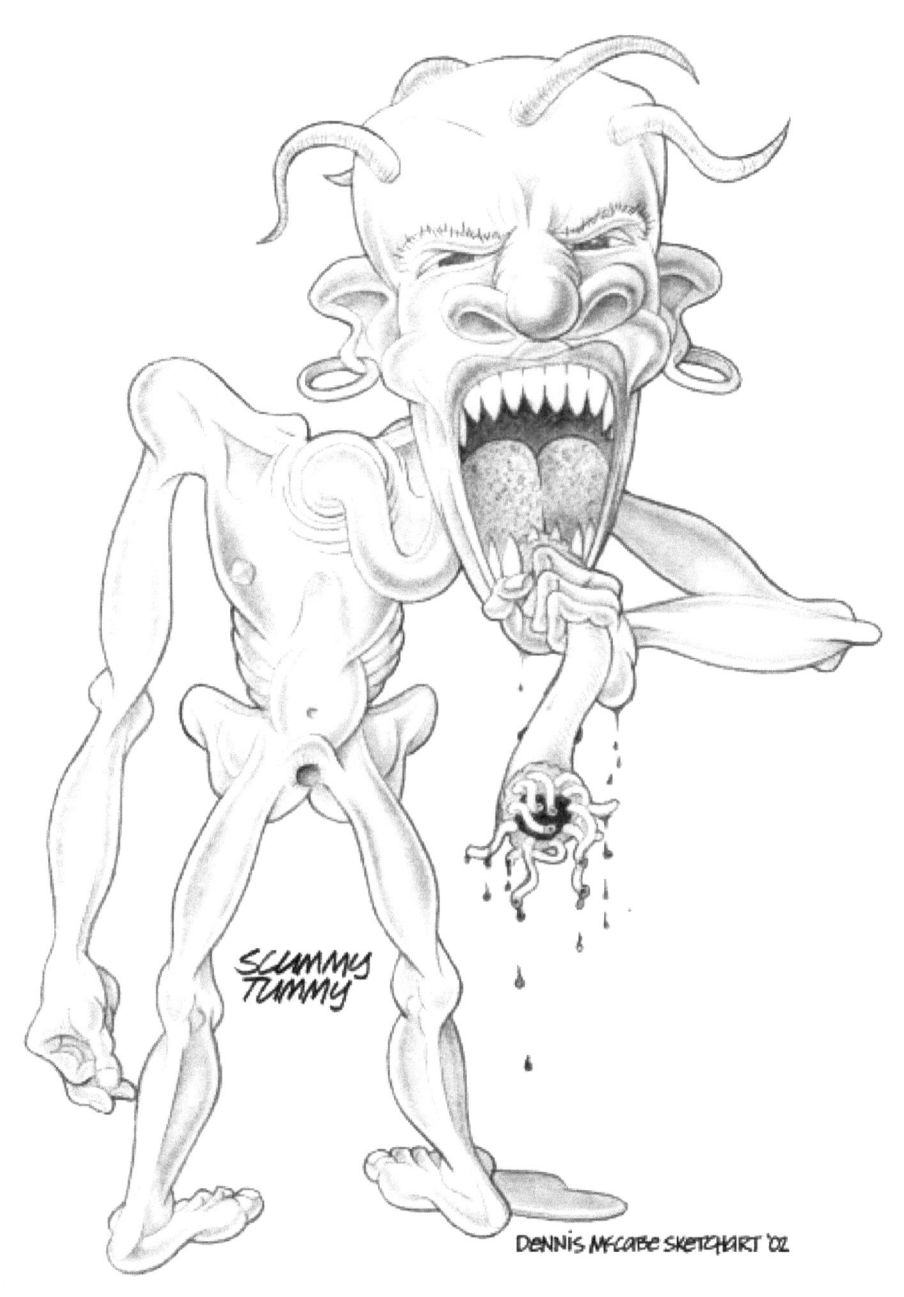

"Scummy Tummy"
Dennis McCabe

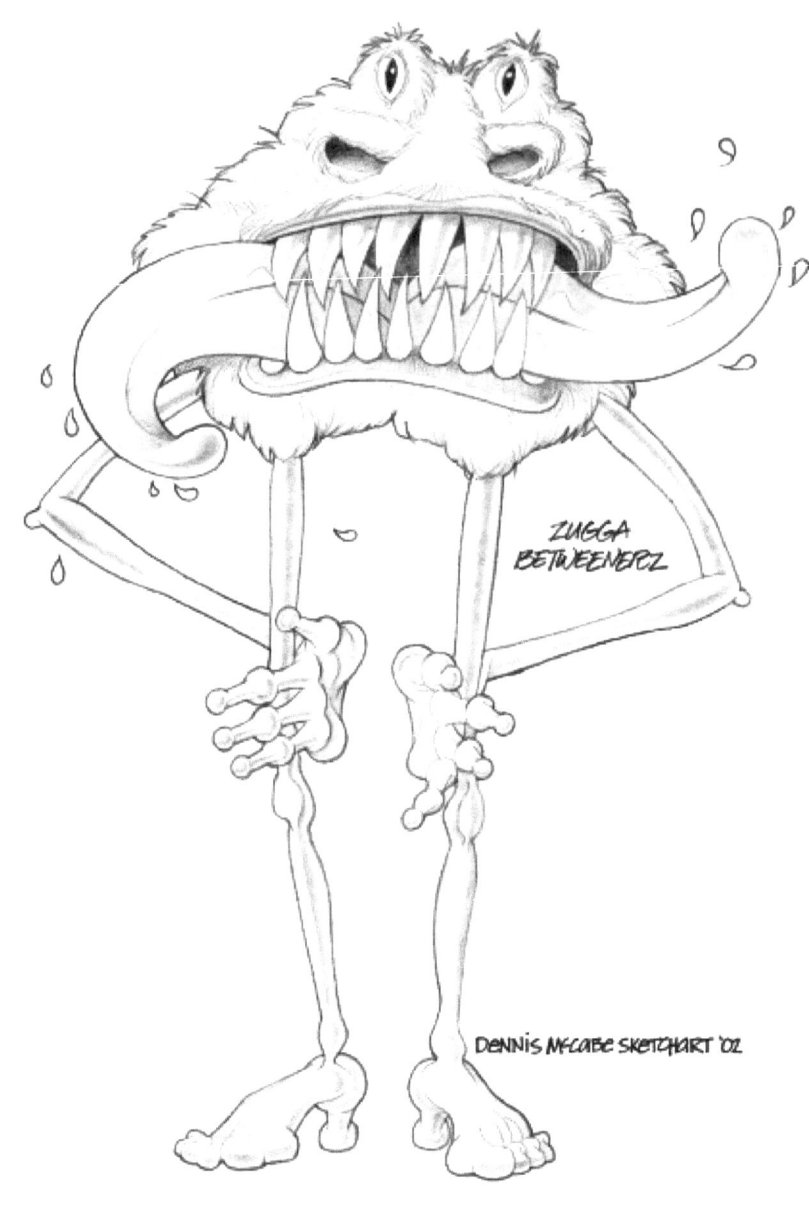

"Zugga Betweenerz"
Dennis McCabe

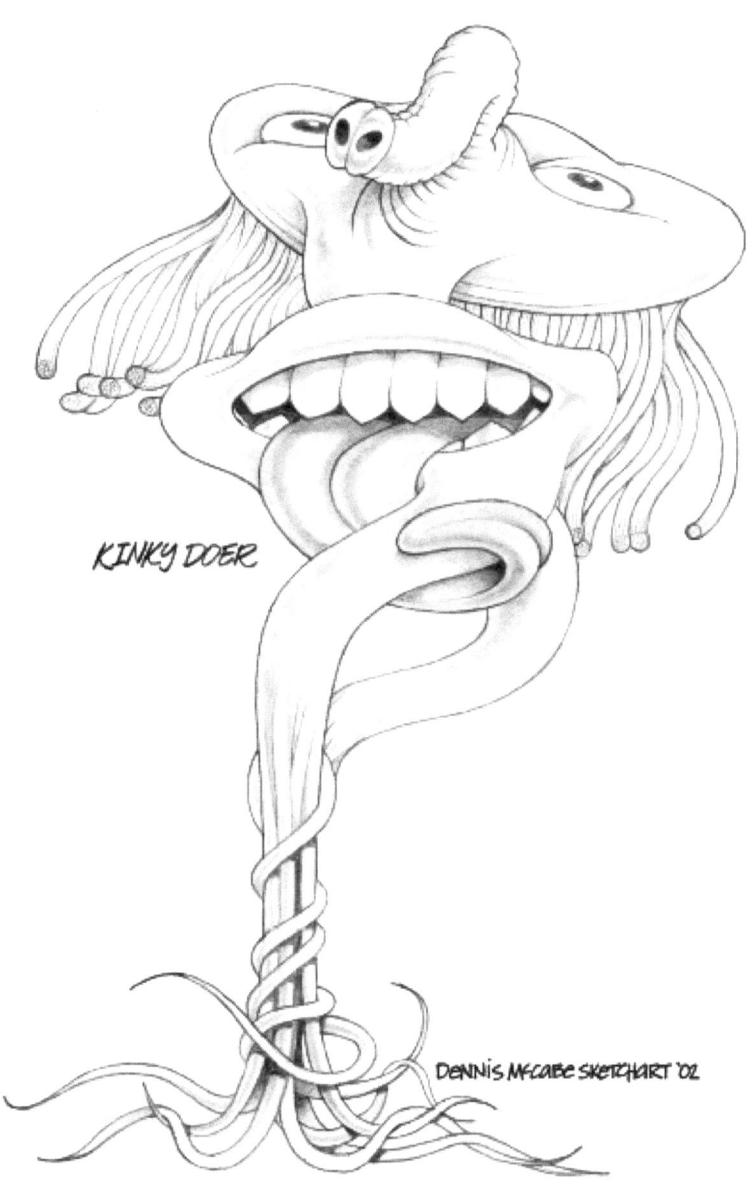

"Kinky Doer"
Dennis McCabe

# Lester Blum

Drawing upon his artistic vision for design, balance, and color, Lester Blum began exploring photography ten years ago. Primarily self taught, his work has been exhibited in numerous juried group shows, published in Kissed, an anthology, received the Sing Si Schwartz Memorial Award for Photography from the Salmagundi Art Club in New York, and is included in private collections.

lesterblumphotography.com

lbphoto18@aol.com

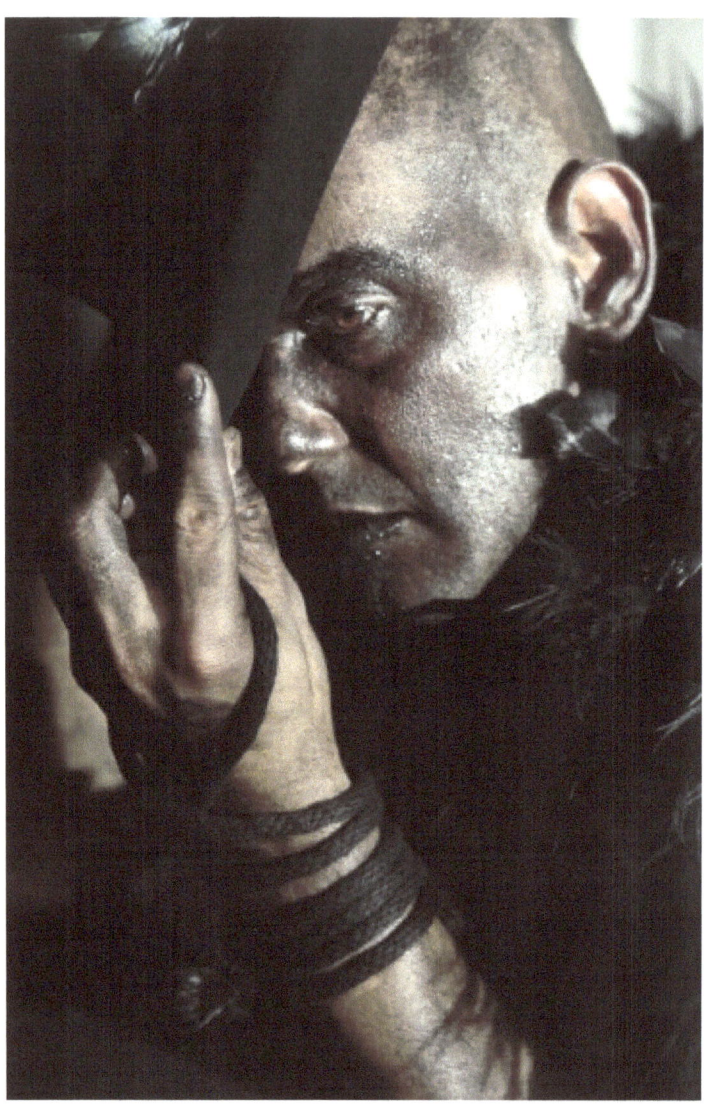

"Voodoo Mystery"
Lester Blum

Model: Vladimir Rios

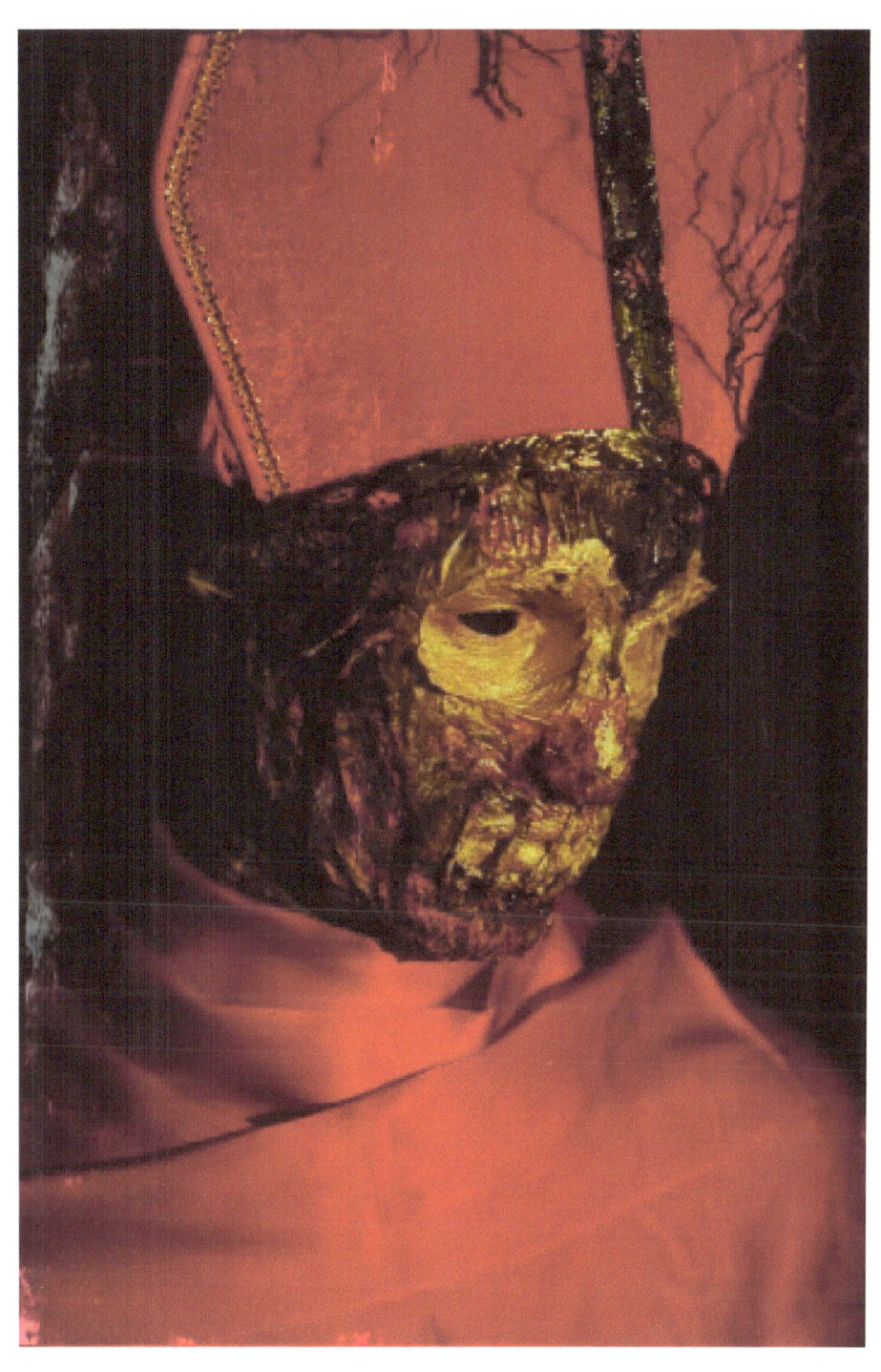

"The Forbidden Curse"
Lester Blum

Concept & MUA:  Dmitry Byalik

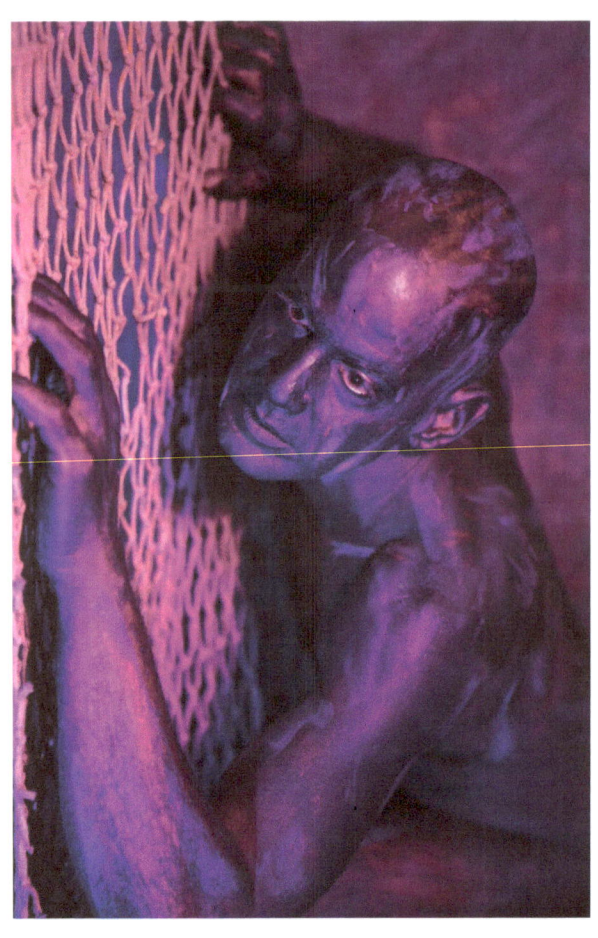

"Climbing Out"
Lester Blum

Model: Vladimir Rios

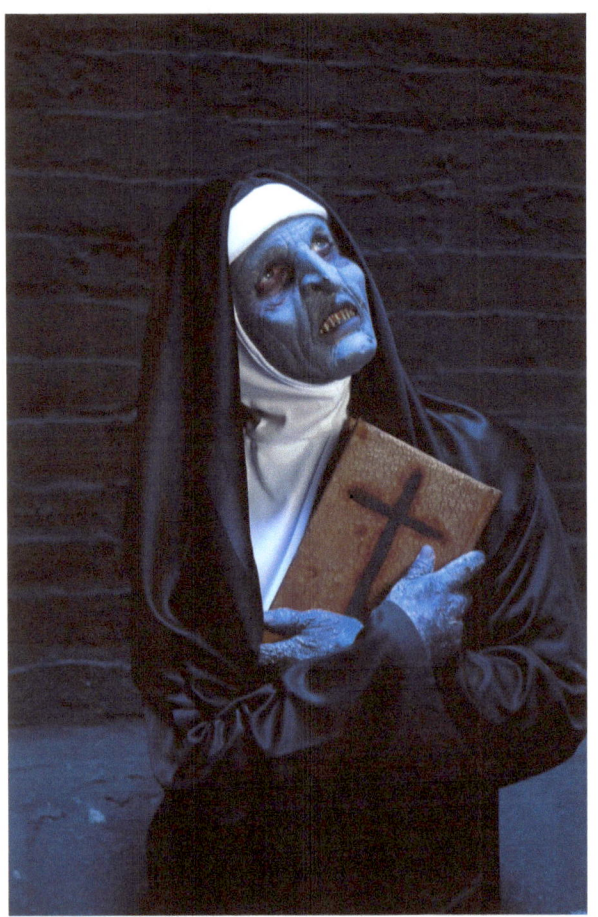

"The Forbidden Curse"
Lester Blum

Concept & MUA: Dmitry Byalik

# Matthew Thompson is a local California artist with high ambition.
He is known in the art community as "Edgy, astounding and gritty."

mthompsonart.deviantart.com/gallery/

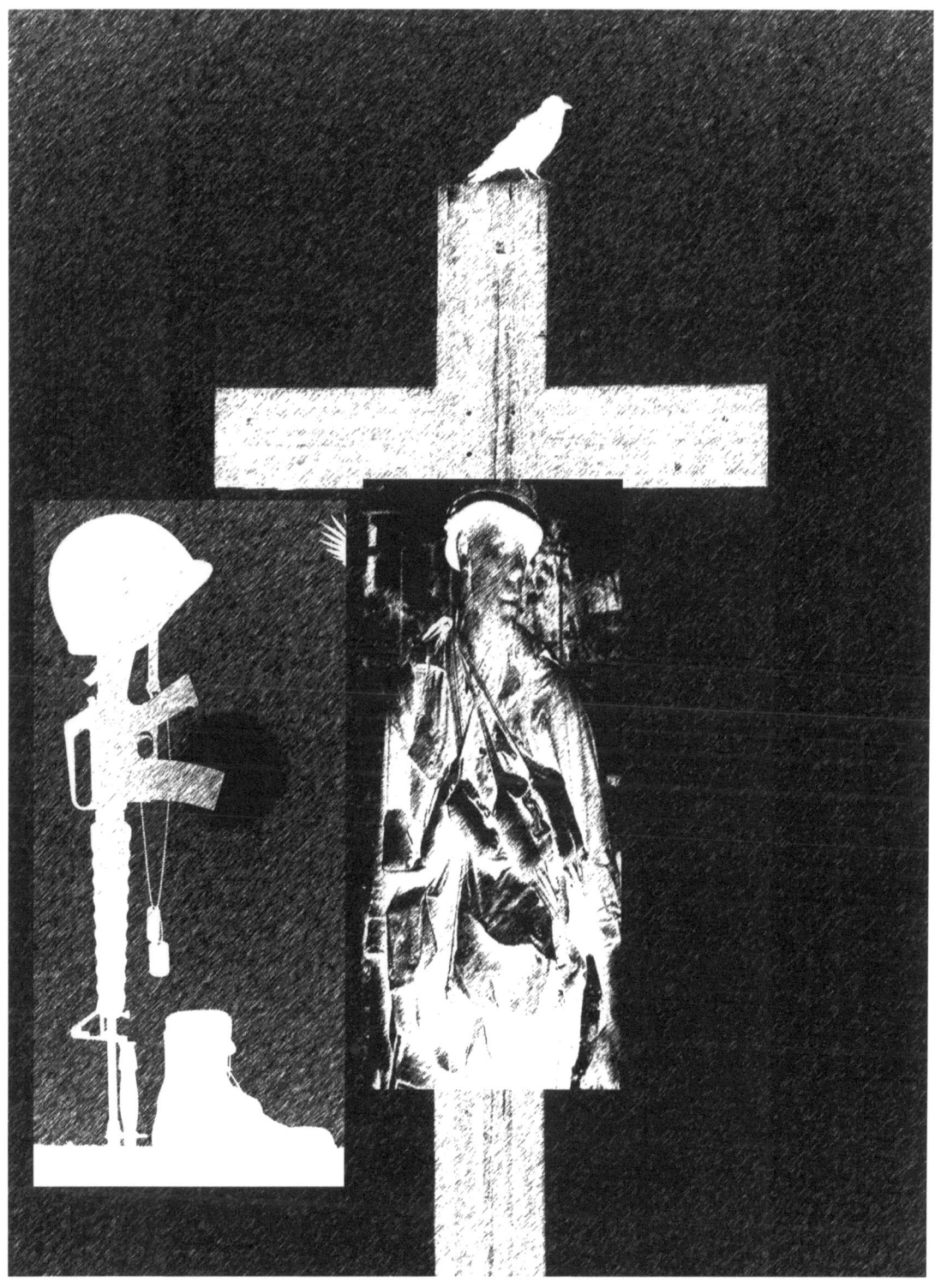

"Dog's Blood Stains, the Crucifiction"
Matthew Thompson

**Nicky Page** is a freelance photographer from northwest Indiana, specializing in nature and portrait photography. She received her certificate upon graduation from NYIP in 2007 and is currently an official photographer for PhotoWorld Magazine.

To see more of her work, please visit Stargazr Photography on EyeEm, Facebook, Flickr, Instagram, Model Mayhem, and Tumblr.

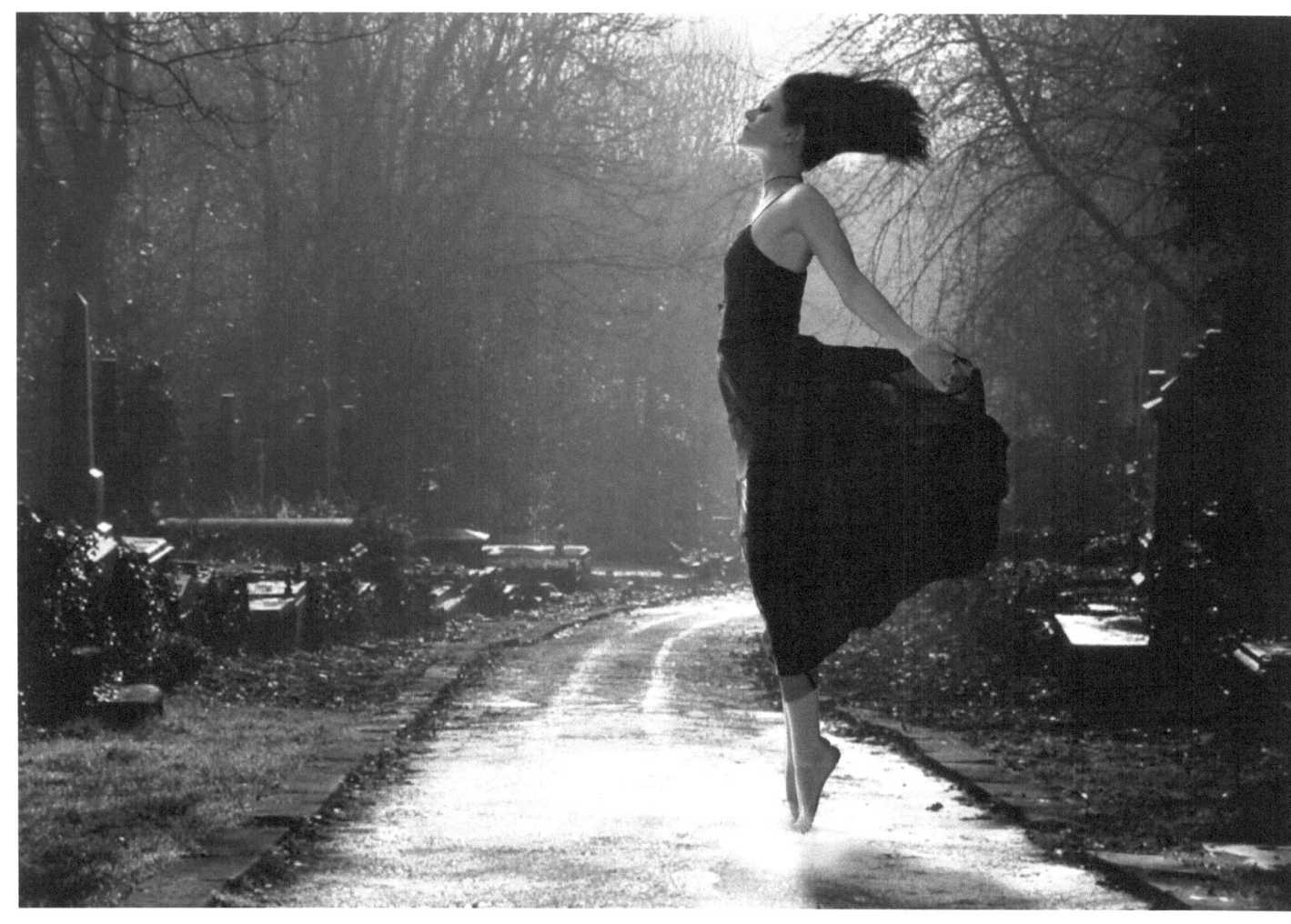

"Cemetery Girl"
Nicky Page
Model: Lora Mercado

# Christina Efkarpides

is a Hellenic artist stationed in Queens, New York. She is a symbolist and allegorical painter and writer. Work includes explorations of psyche and spirituality with an incline toward the metaphysical. Work portrays an unseen reality, while being depicted as another realm heavily influenced by the afterlife and the underworld. Formally a 'cadaver restoration specialist' stationed in south Florida sparked a deep interest in the afterlife, ritual, and spirit.

fineartamerica.com/profiles/Nina-christy.html

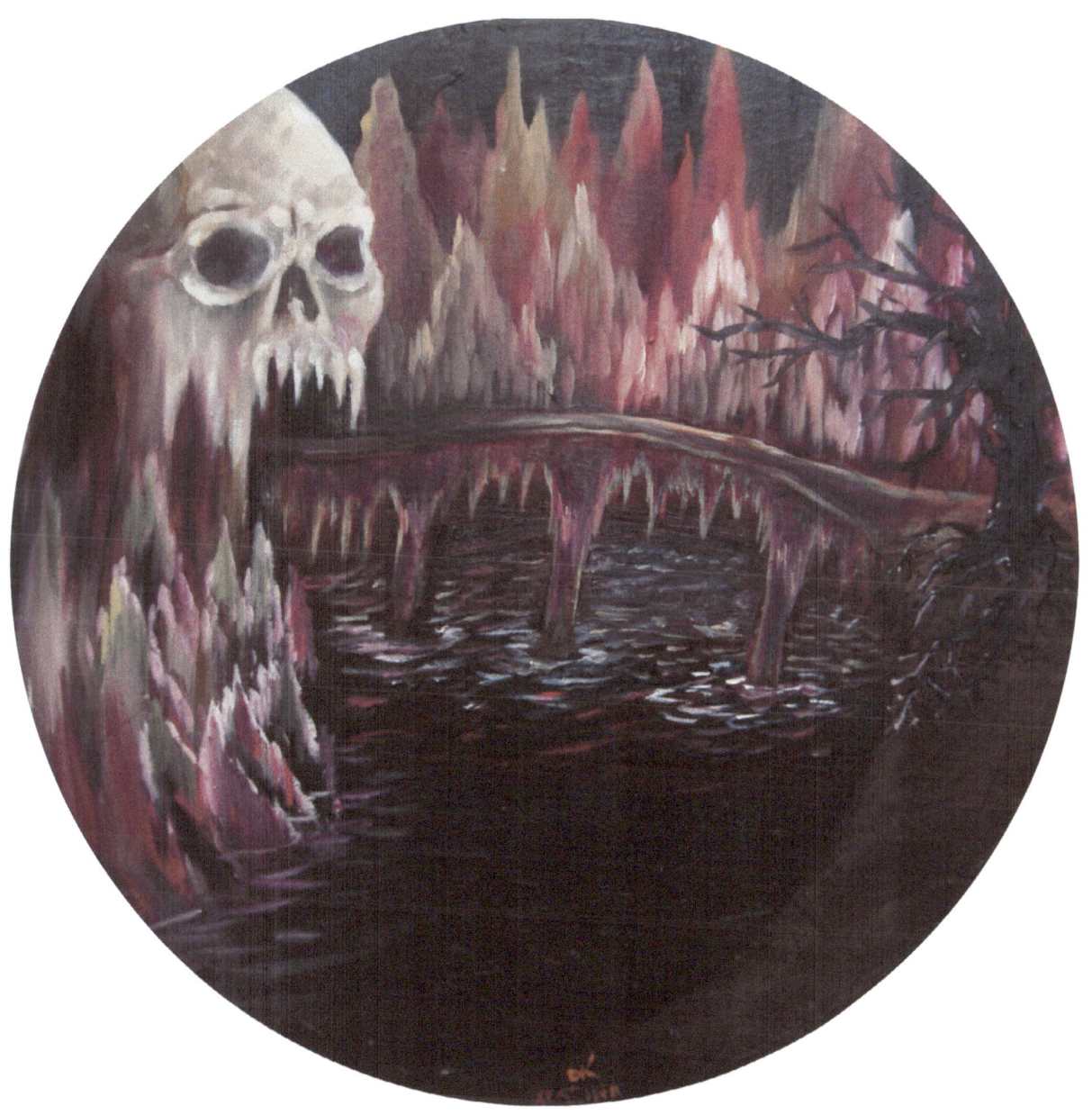

"Skull Bridge"
Christina Efkarpides

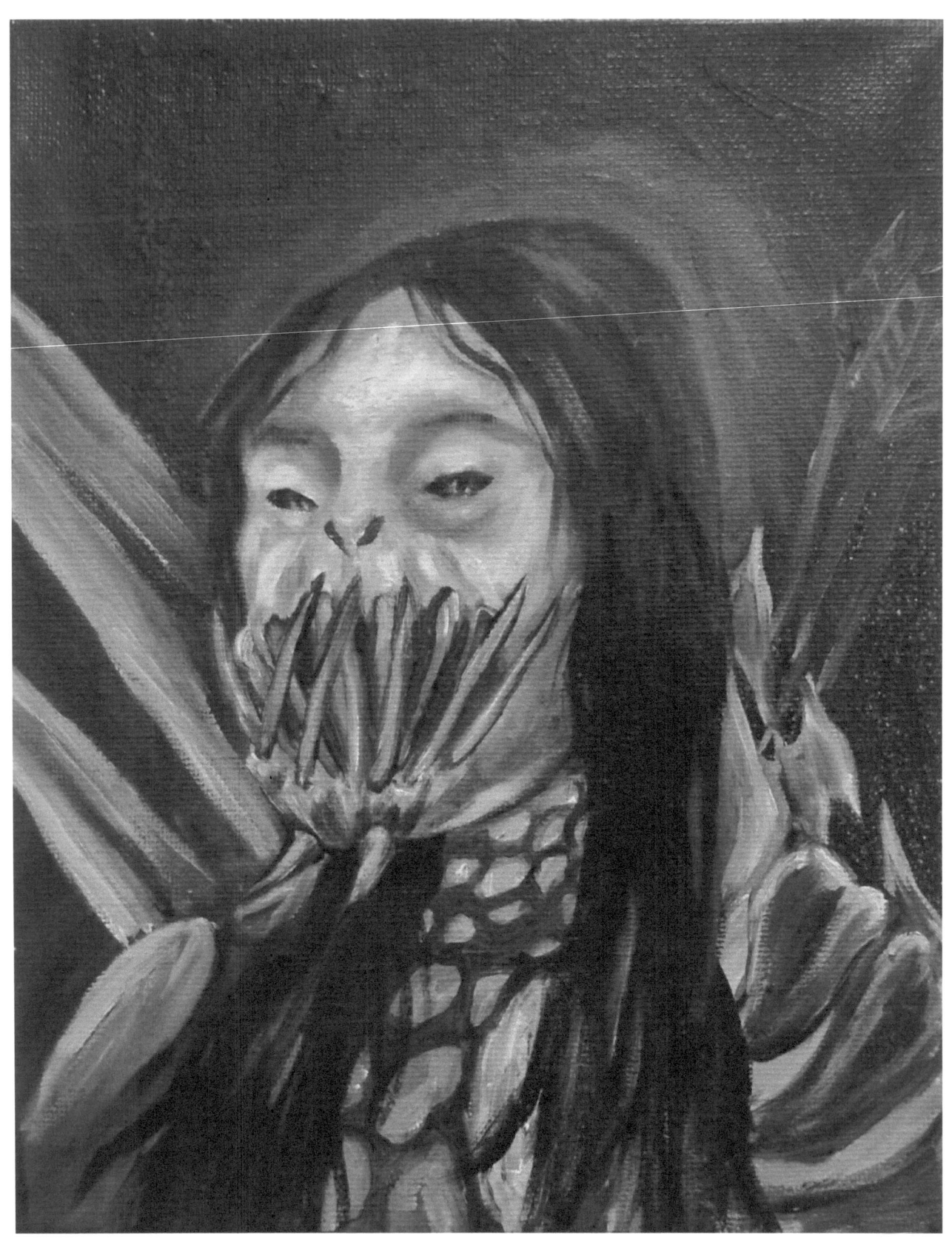

"Alien Hunter"
Christina Efkarpides

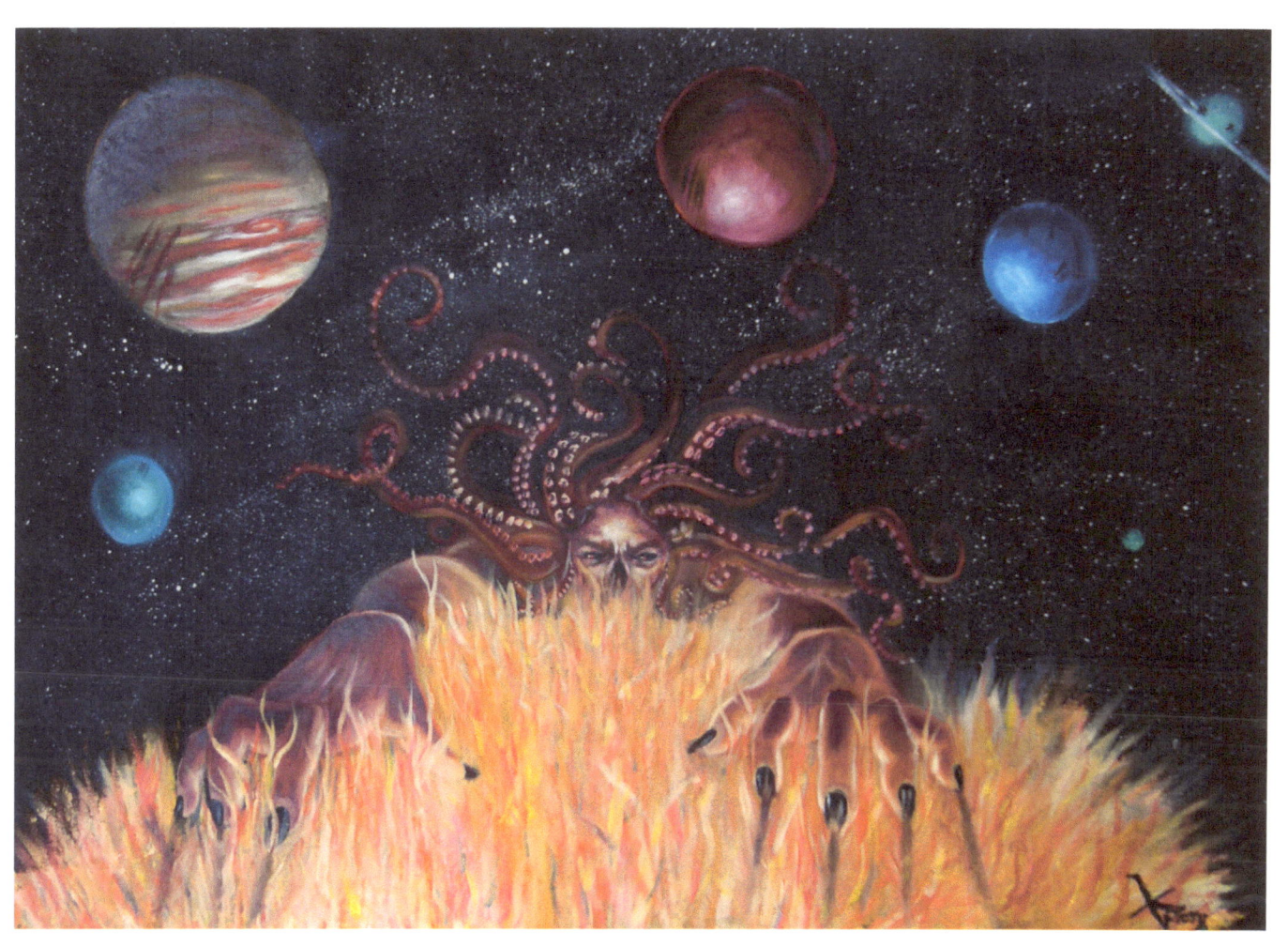

"ReCreating"
Christina Efkarpides

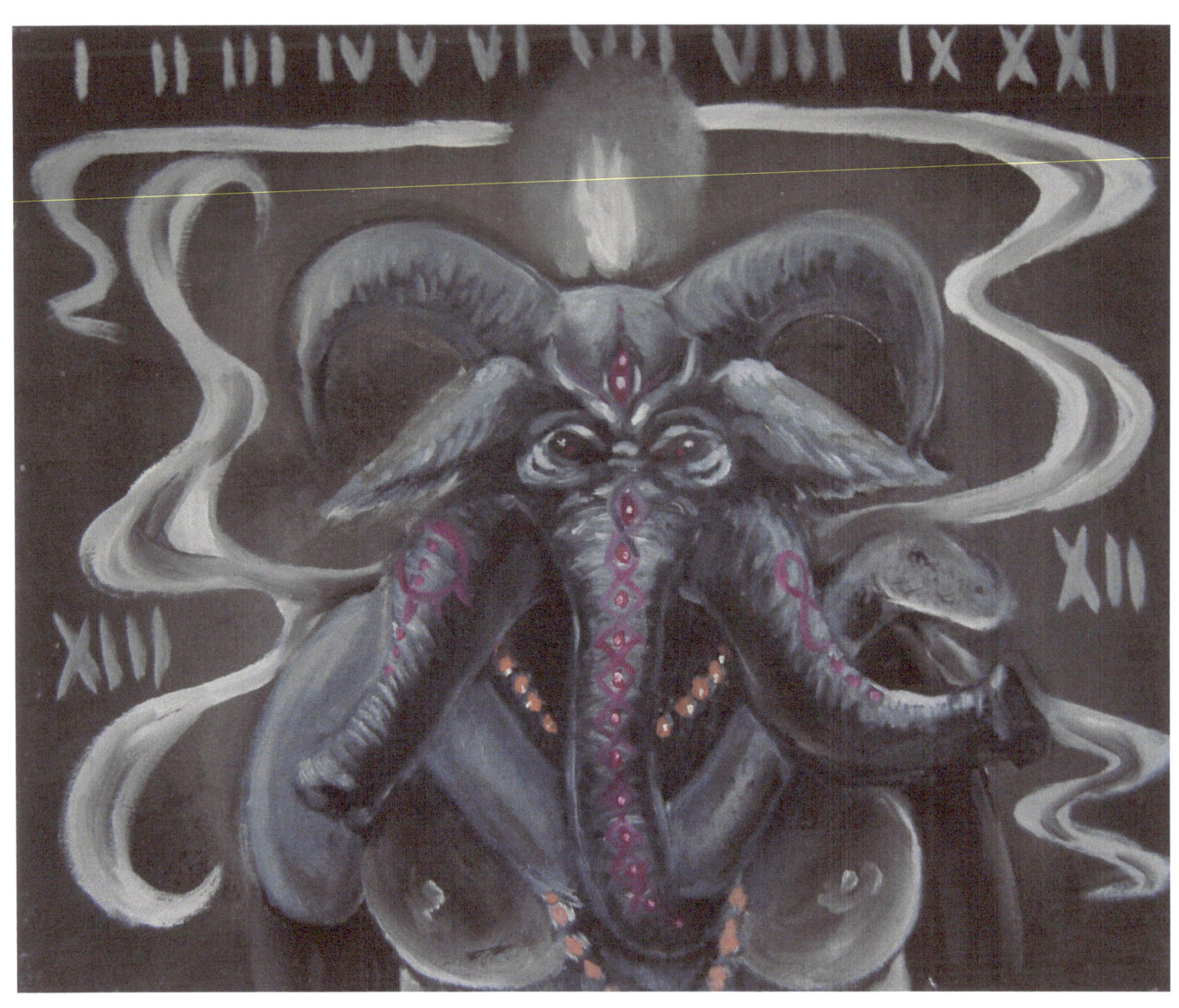

"Satan's Ganesha"
Christina Efkarpides

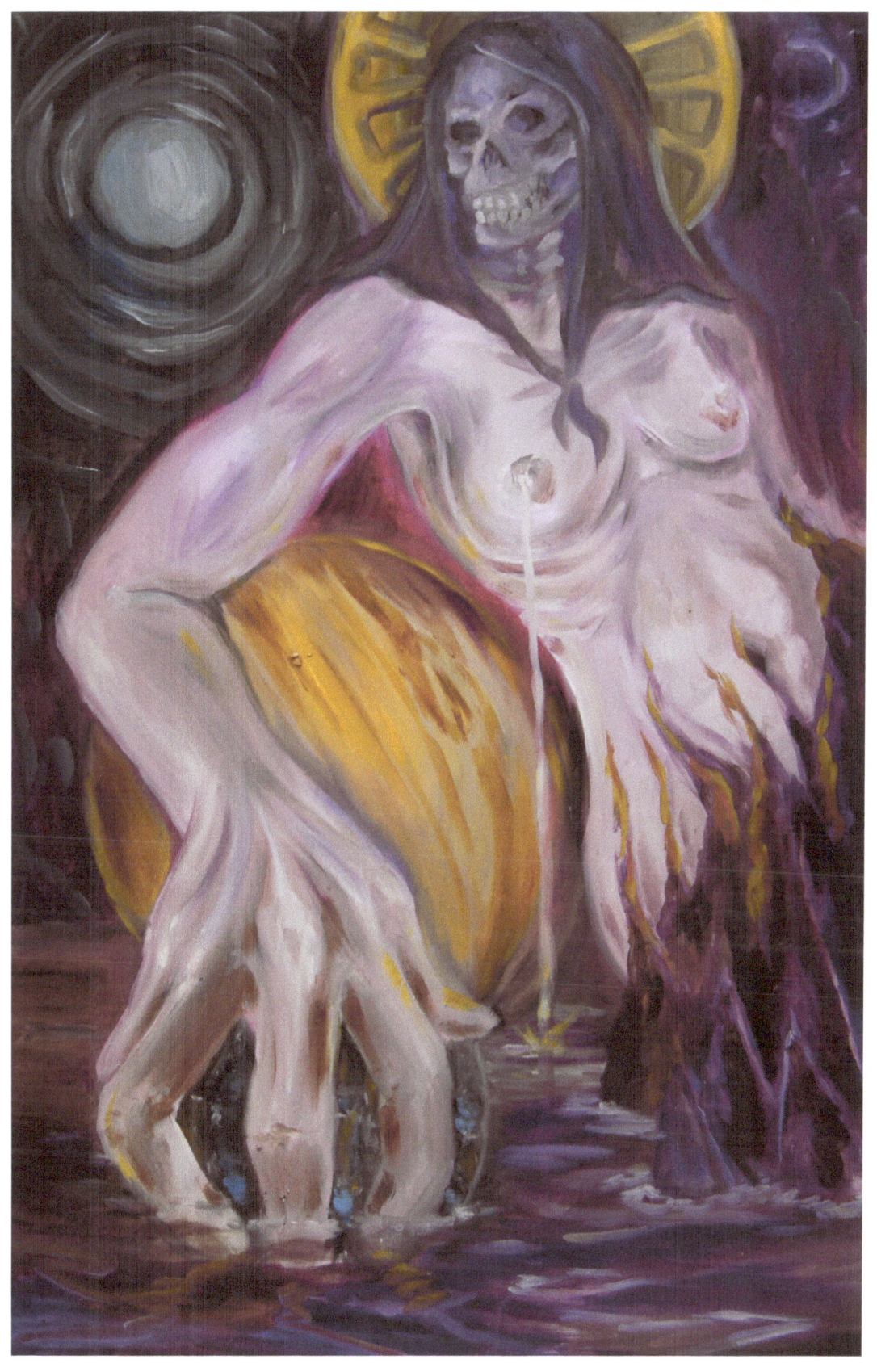

"Saint Mother Death"
Christina Efkarpides

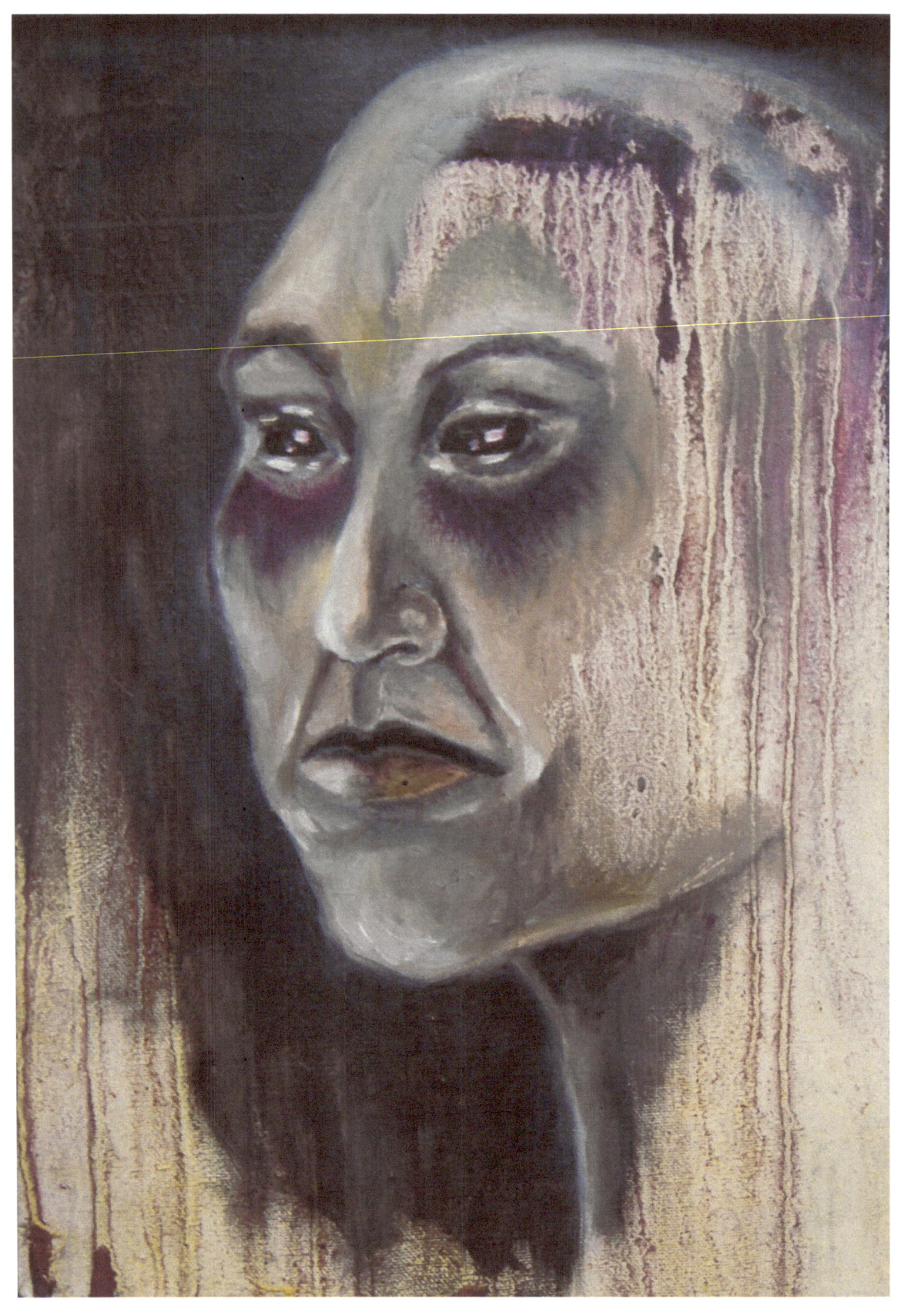

"Alien Drip"
Christina Efkarpides

# Camilla Beenaux

I consider my art to be a window into the darkest corners of my mind. Images conjured up by ugly memories. Things that frightened me as a child. Those oft imagined and other times legitimate ghouls that lurk between the pages of everyone's life story. The past is a powerful beast and I try my hardest to capture that on paper.

I am a self-taught artist who began drawing in the winter of 2011 when a friend handed me a gel pen and a piece of notebook paper and I haven't stopped for a moment since then. I consider every line, colour, and spot to be a satisfying chunk of "emotional vomit" from within. Every piece is created spontaneously, beginning merely as a line that then takes me on a journey of marker strokes and sharpie dots, which is generally finished within twenty to thirty minutes, at a rate of three to four drawings per day. My medium of choice is the ever mighty sharpie and pen, however I will from time to time dabble in acrylics.

camillabeenaux.com

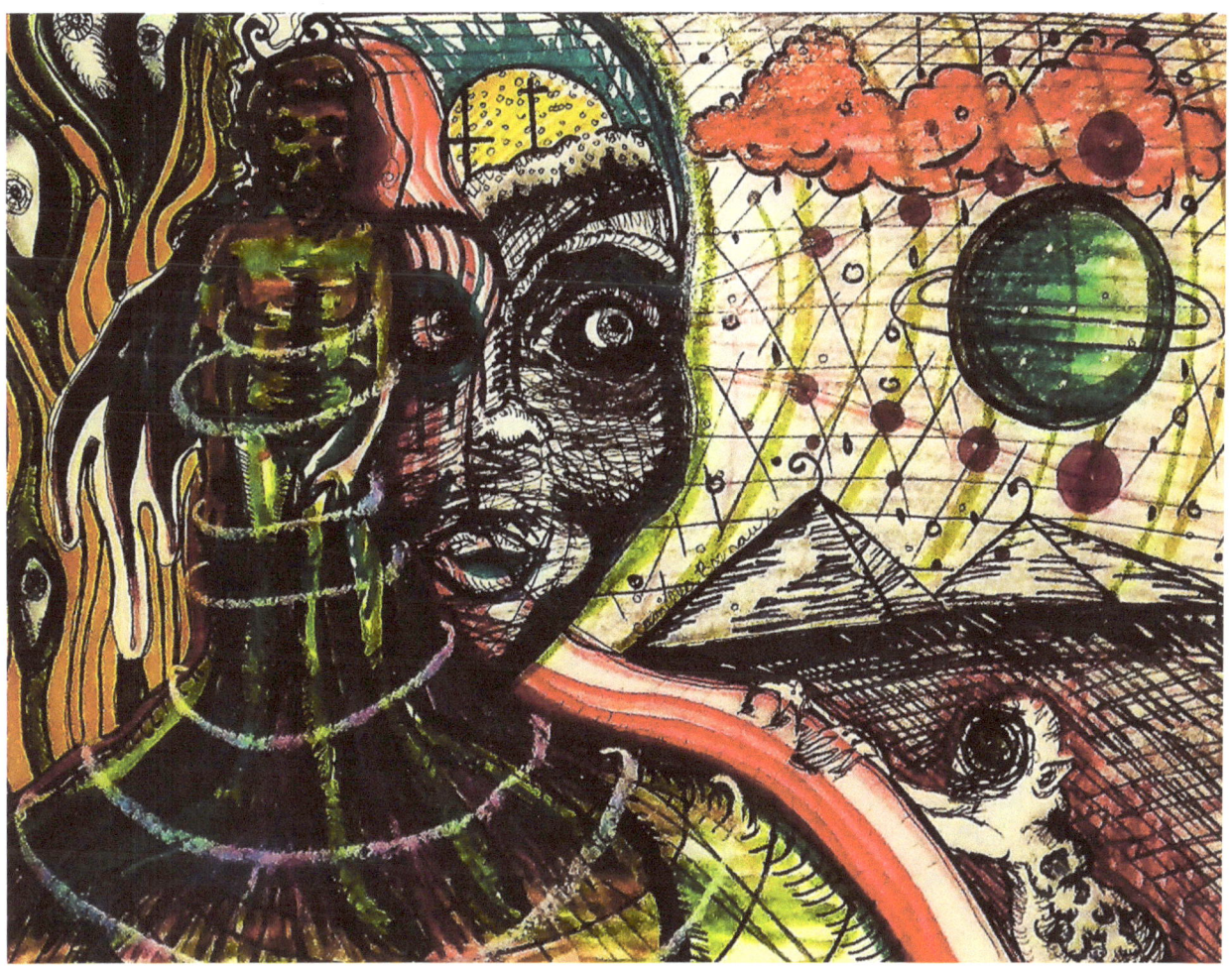

"No Place Like Home"
Camilla Beenaux

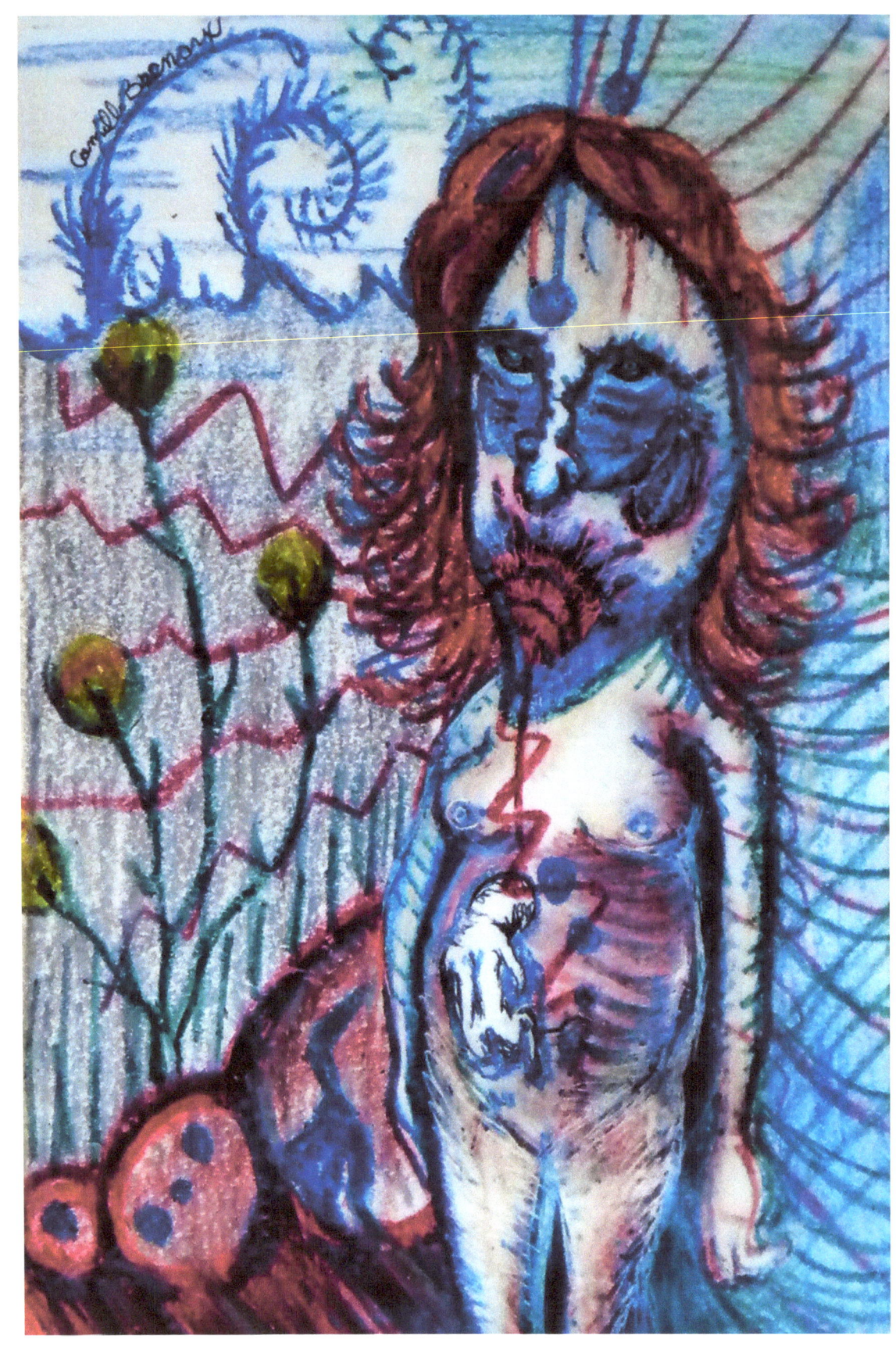

"Alien Beginnings"
Camilla Beenaux

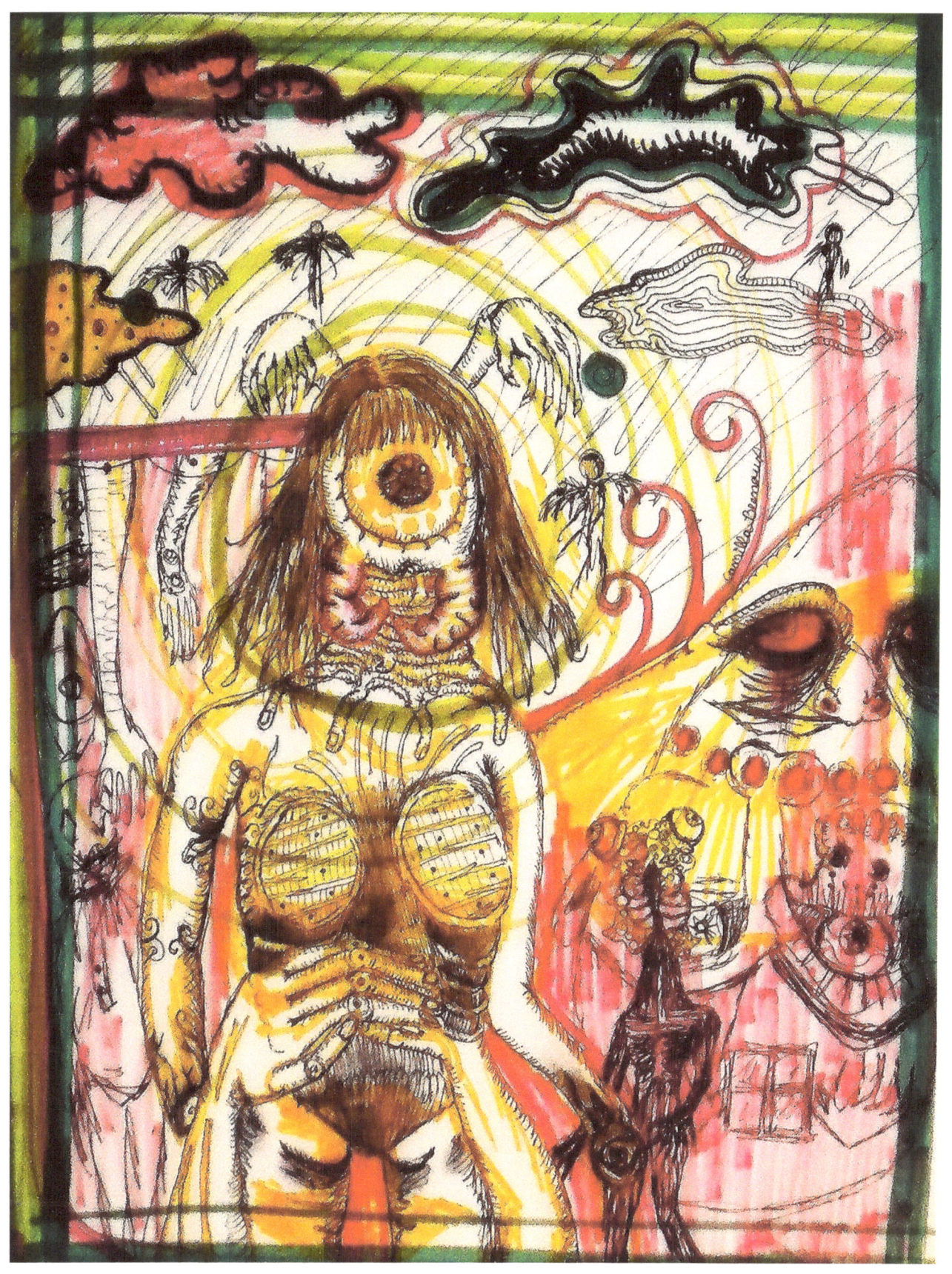

"Beauty Queen"
Camilla Beenaux

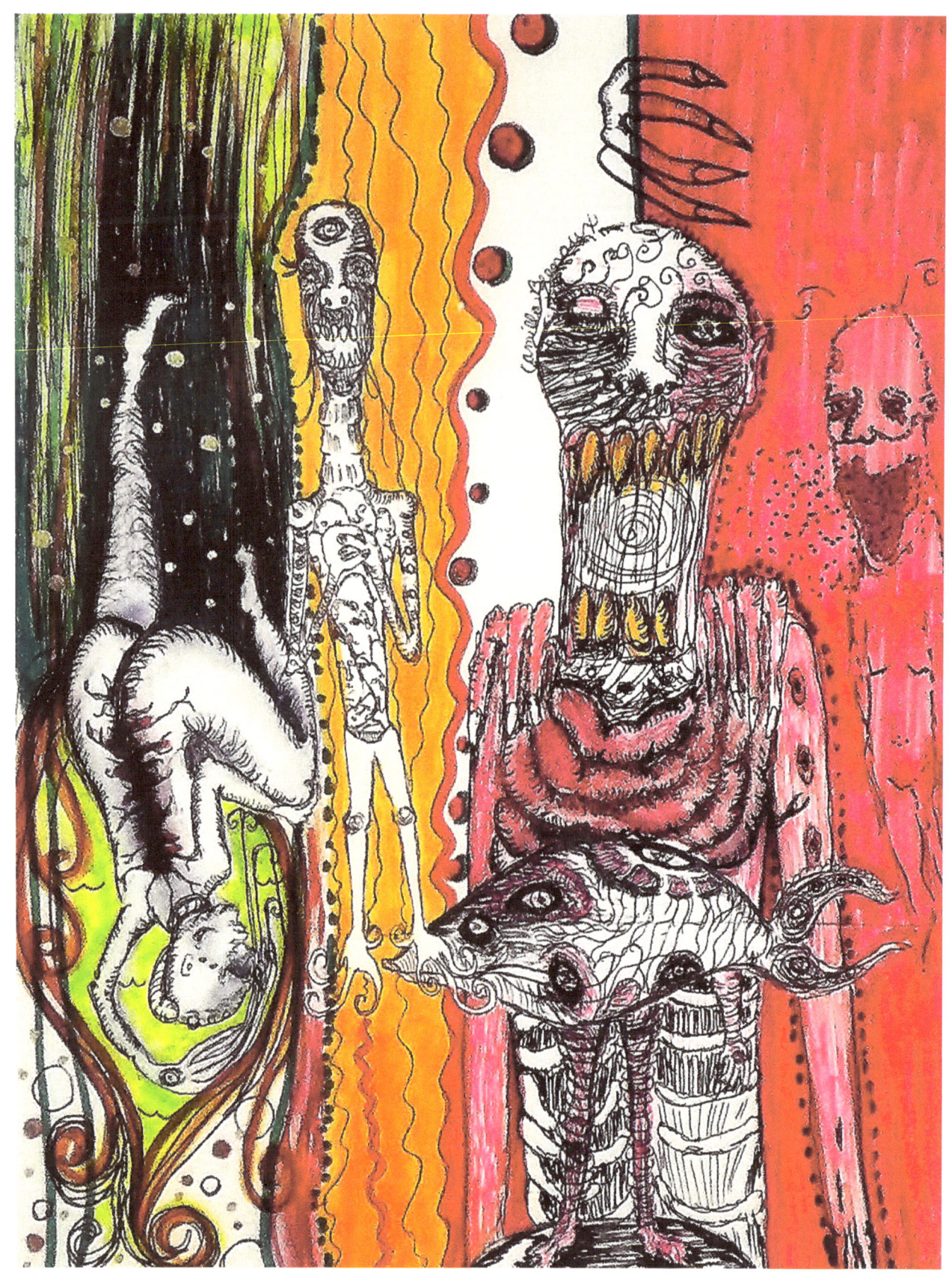

"Sonic Hole"
Camilla Beenaux

# Matthew Hester

Growing up with artists in my family I have seen various styles of Beautiful work of the years. My aunt who is an established painter, taught me to open my mind and see the world in many shades of colors. While my father gave me the gift to capture life and in many ways death through the eye of a lens.

While I chose to pursue photography, I also tried to take what I learned from my aunt and incorporate it into my my work. When I shoot a picture I try image what a person may be thinking, or what history may beheld in an old building. I always found it fascinating how many different scenarios can run through my head before I give it the final click of the shutter.

Over the couple years it has been my goal and passion to bring to life the history of once was. Whether it is an old run down state hospital, or a abandoned gun factory, I feel it is important to recognize and pay credence to places that shaped the lives of so many. That is not to say I don't enjoy the love for a bright city skyline or a couple holding hands.

No matter what the case, a photograph can tell so many stories. With a single image so many thoughts can be had. It really is left the imagination of the viewer when all is said and done, and that is what I strive for. I want people to look at my work and ask what may lead down that dark creepy hallway, or what that cabby eating a hot dog is pondering about.

matthewhester.com

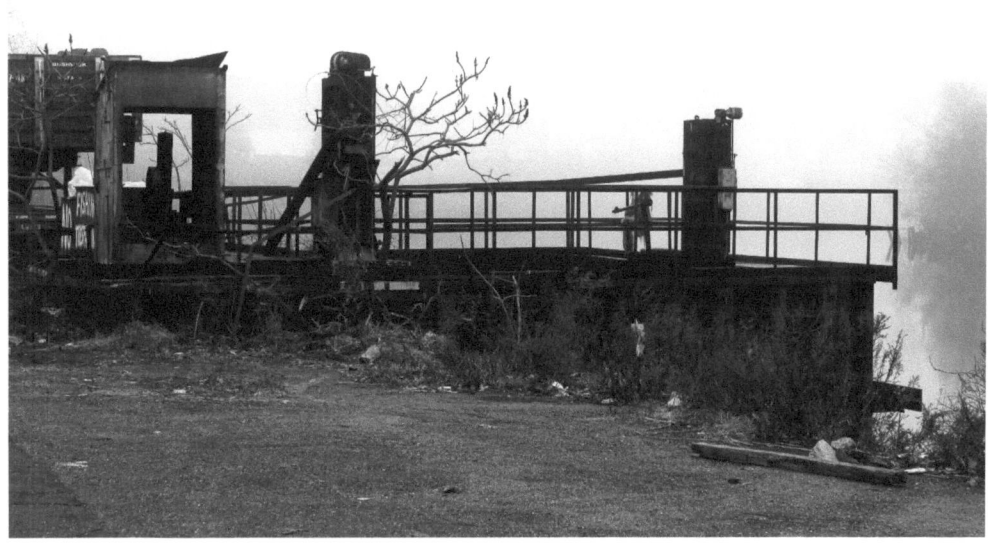

"Lost in the Fog"
Matthew Hester

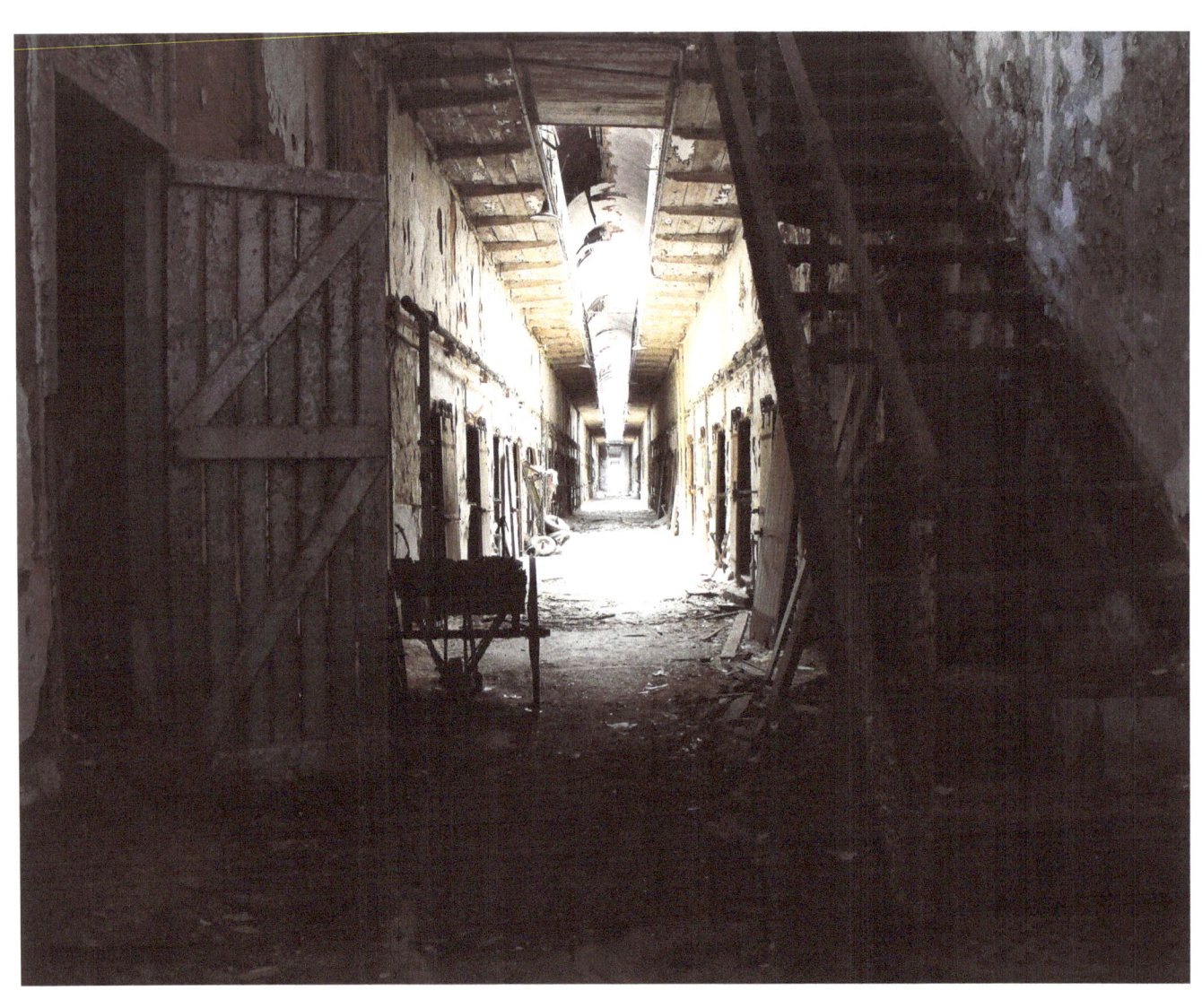

"Eastern State Penetentiary"
Matthew Hester

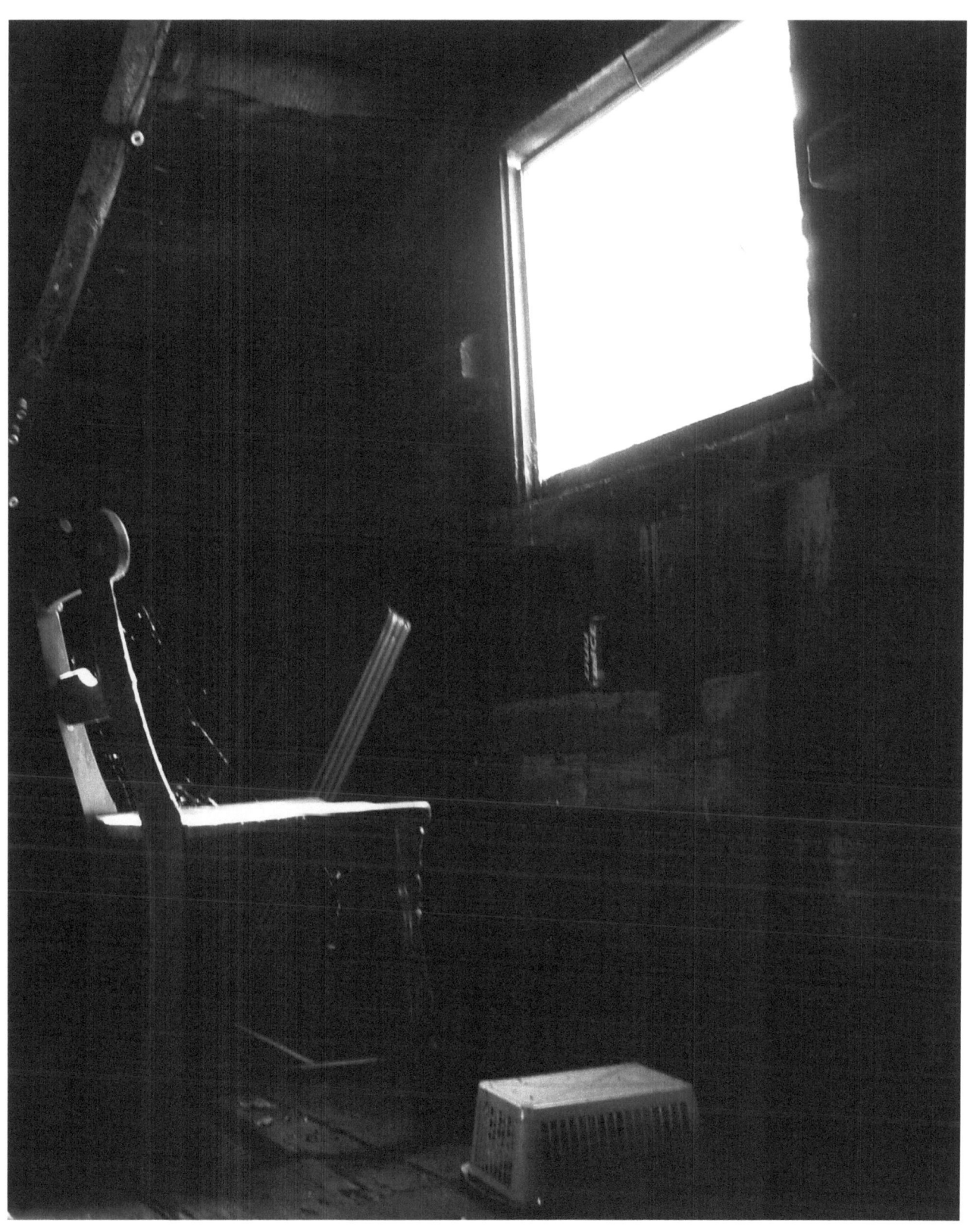

"Sunrise Resort Final Chapter"
Matthew Hester

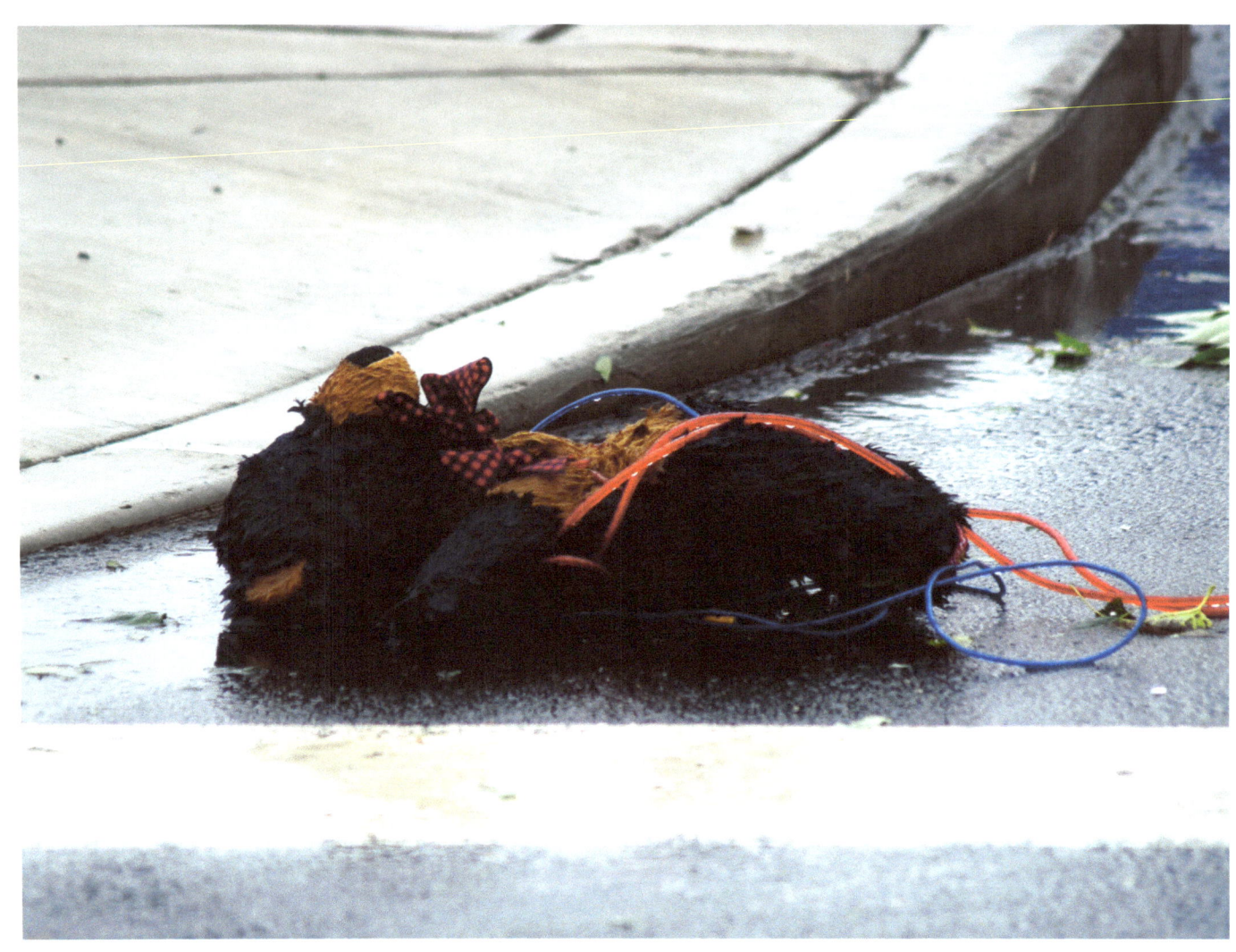

"Lost Friend"
Matthew Hester

# Brian Matheny

The paintings explore a self-imposed ambiguity, angst without glamour, doubting barrenness, historical and symbolic endeavors to identify man's ineptitude. A culture's final ruse. The paintings grimace with dissonance and a foreboding distinctiveness, denied faculties characterized by genuineness obscured by modern/now/consumption/fame/fragmented/no more questions/…a life of nauseating, replicating, and anticipating successions of lifeless and empty values used in denying a self-inflicted psychosis. Pinning contemporary uncertainty/obscenities/ugliness personified by fashionable societal agendas. They are a self crumbling hopelessly in redemption.

brianpmatheny.tumblr.com

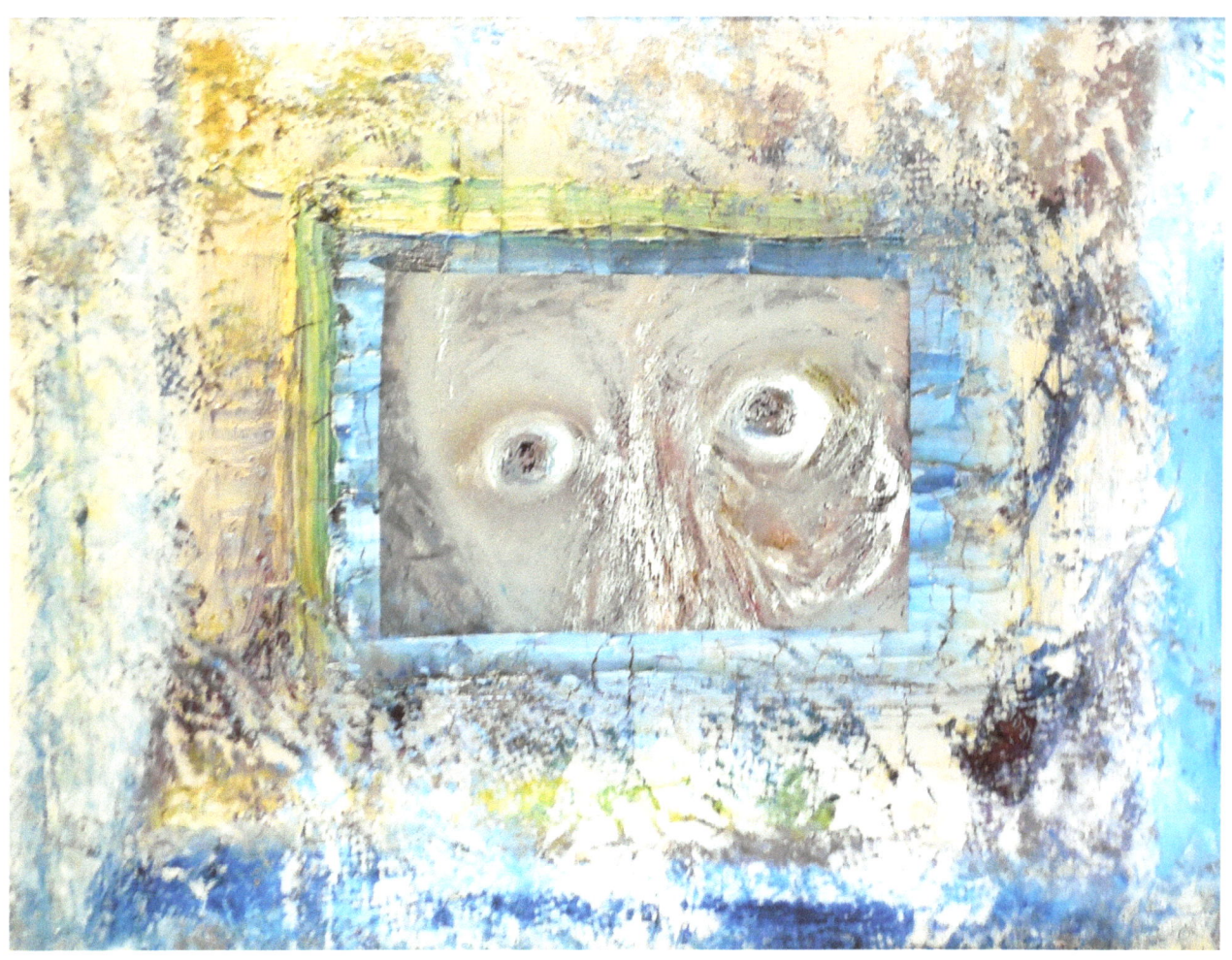

"Avoidance"
Brian Matheny

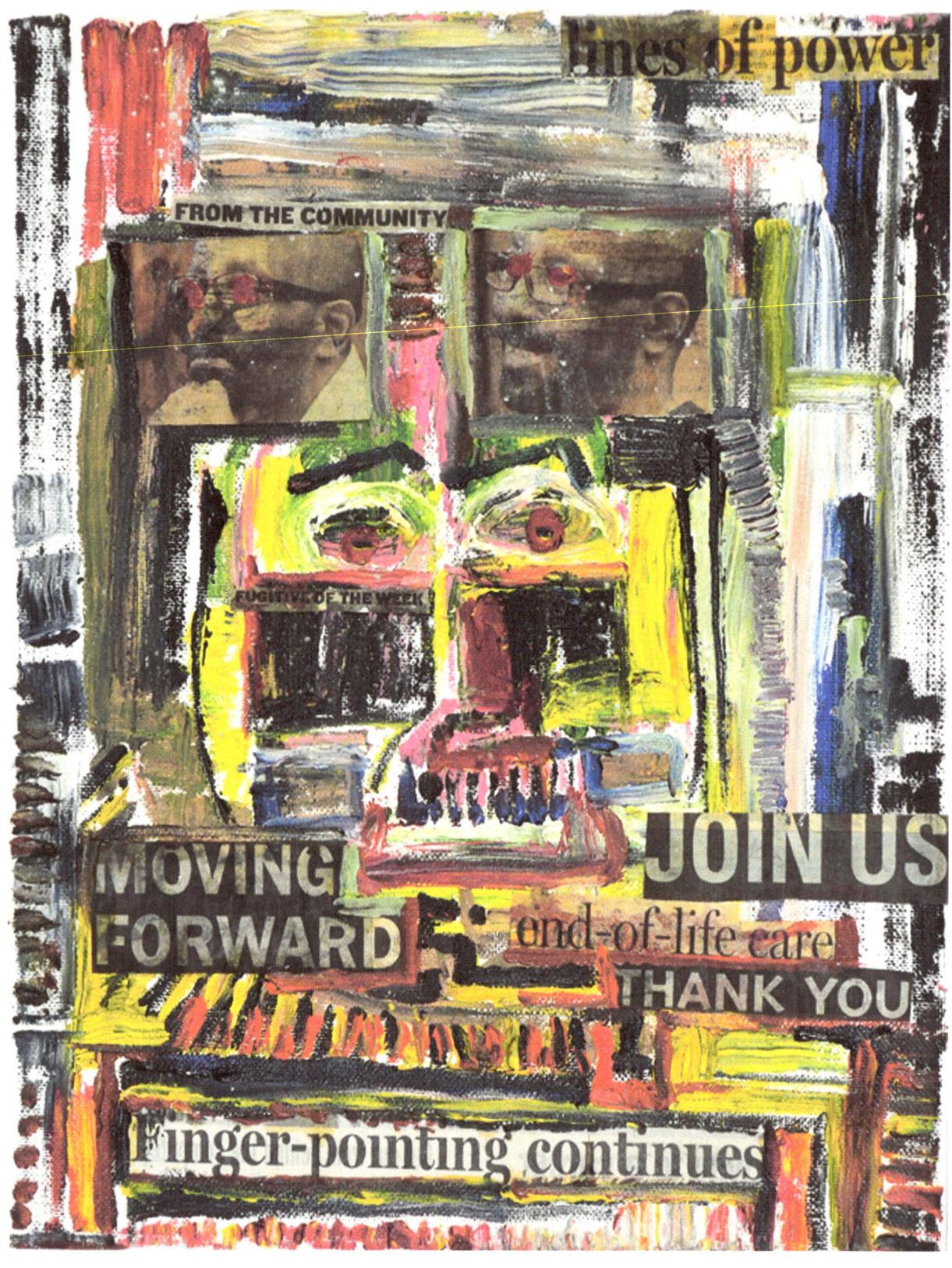

"Community"
Brian Matheny

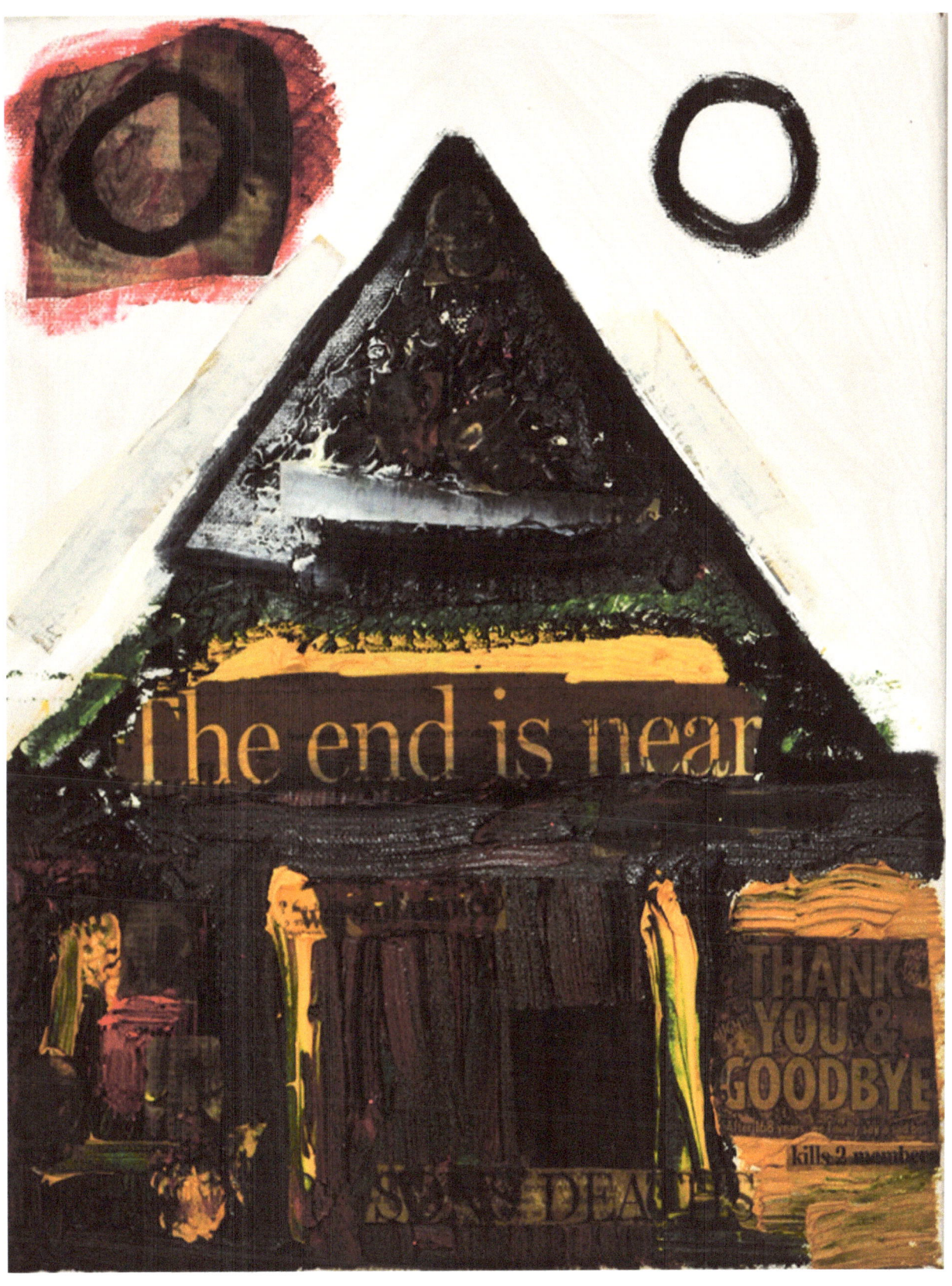

"Goodbye"
Brian Matheny

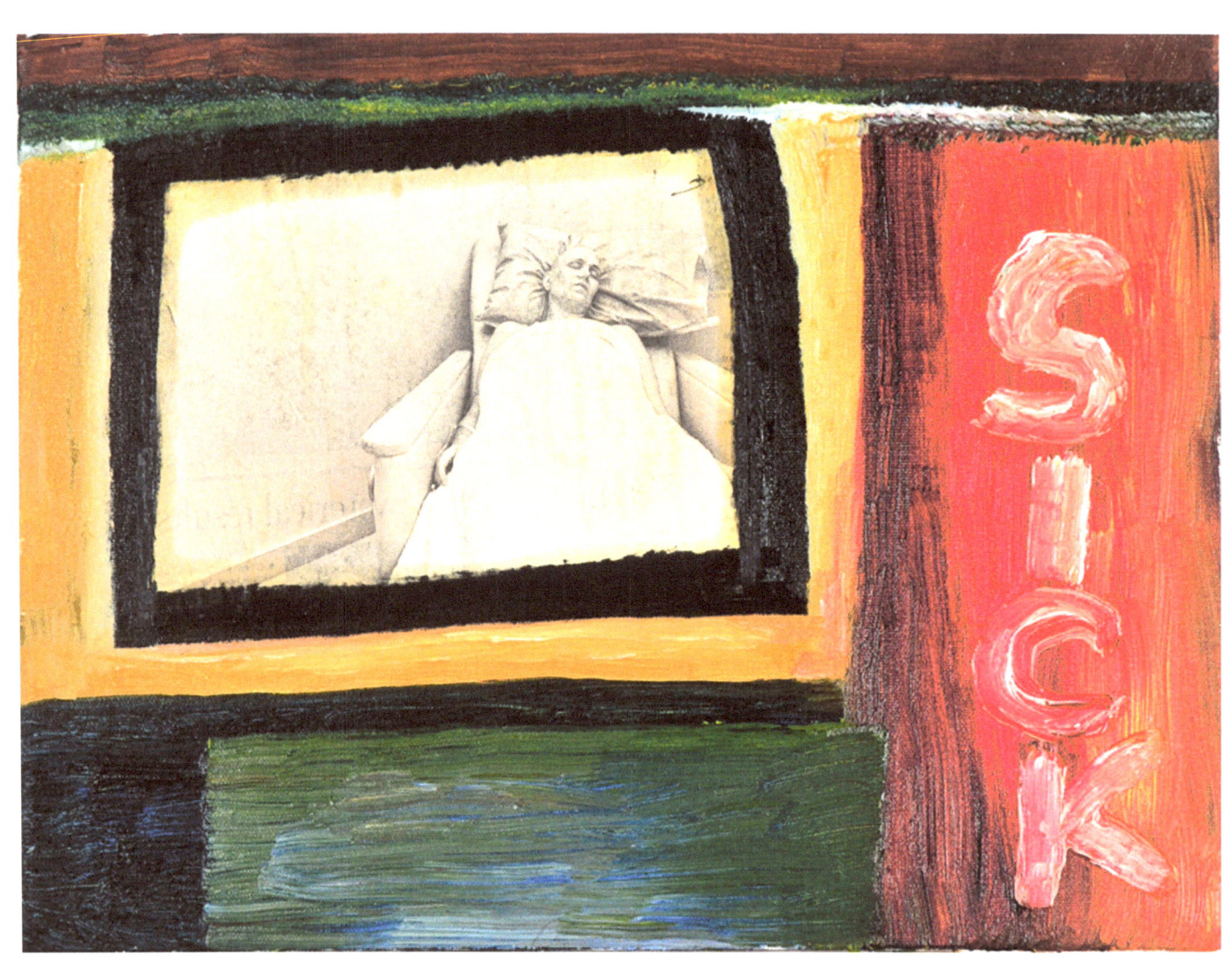

"Sick"
Brian Matheny

**Jeff Martin** is the CEO and principal designer at Flawless Enterprises LLC, a creative design and business development consultancy based in Western Kentucky. Until 2012, Jeff's work primarily focused on the commercial applications of graphic and website design in terms of visual branding and publishing. As his business began to shift in its client base, attracting other creative professionals, artists, writers, musicians, etc., the scope of his work also broadened to include a variety of photography and fine arts processes and pursuits. While working with a client to design series of book covers, Jeff developed the concept for his more artistically focused venture under the heading of Marc Prince Productions. Marc Prince signified a revolution in Jeff's professional focus and tremendous freedom, turning the tables of business dictating art to art dictating business.

jeff@flawelssenterprises.us

http://www.marcprince.co  Marc Prince Productions Website
http://www.flawlessenterprises.us  Flawless Enterprises Website

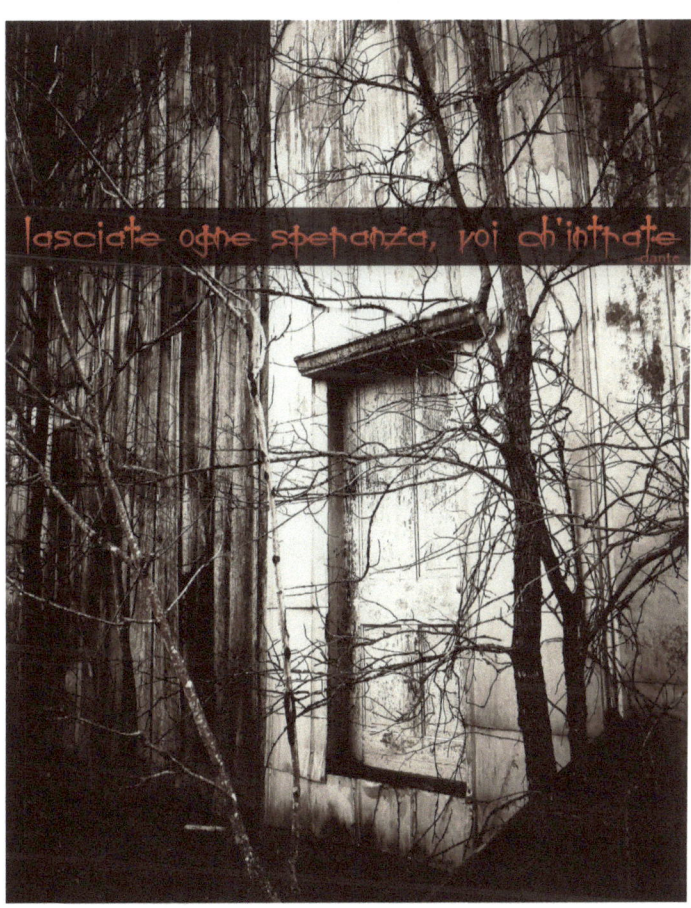

"Inferno"
Jeff Martin

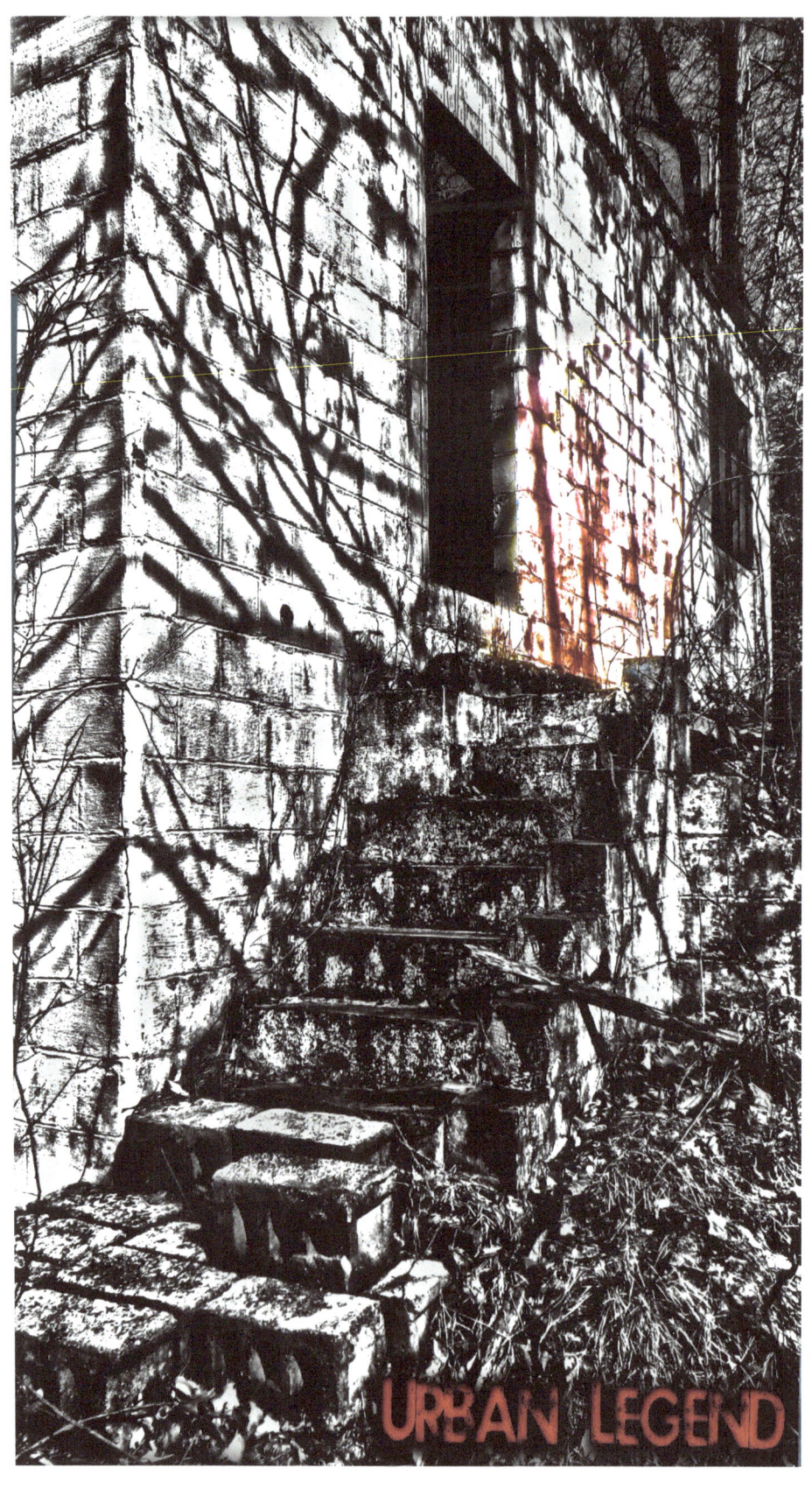

"Urban Legend"
Jeff Martin

# Piper Robbins
is an American born photographer from Sounthern Indiana. She has always felt passionately about photography, and in particular analogue photography. Robbins got her BFA in Photography in San Francisco, CA. She is now a resident of Chicago, where she works full time with film, and analogue photography.

piperrobbins.com

piperrobbins.tumblr.com

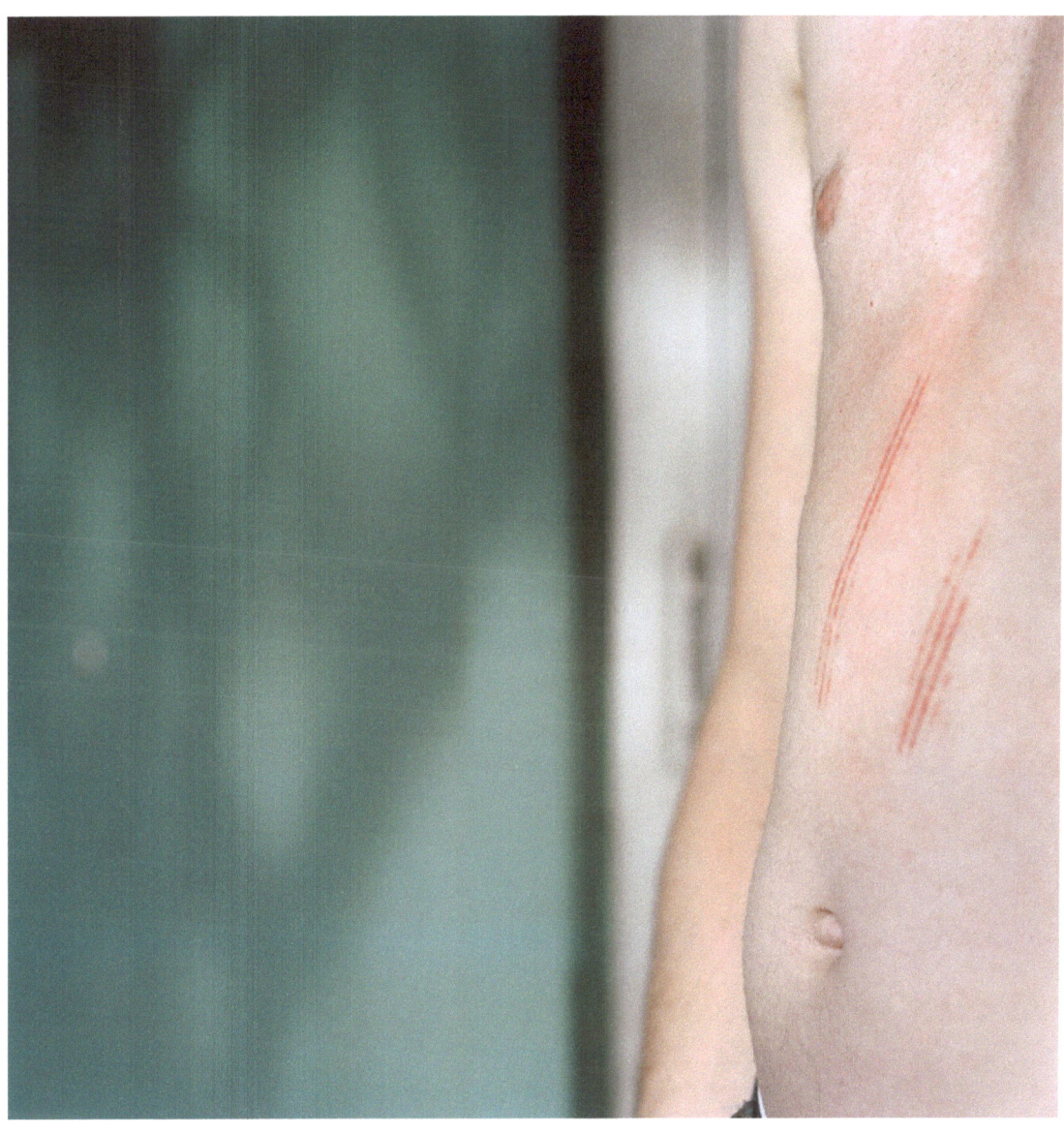

"Belly Scratches"
Piper Robbins

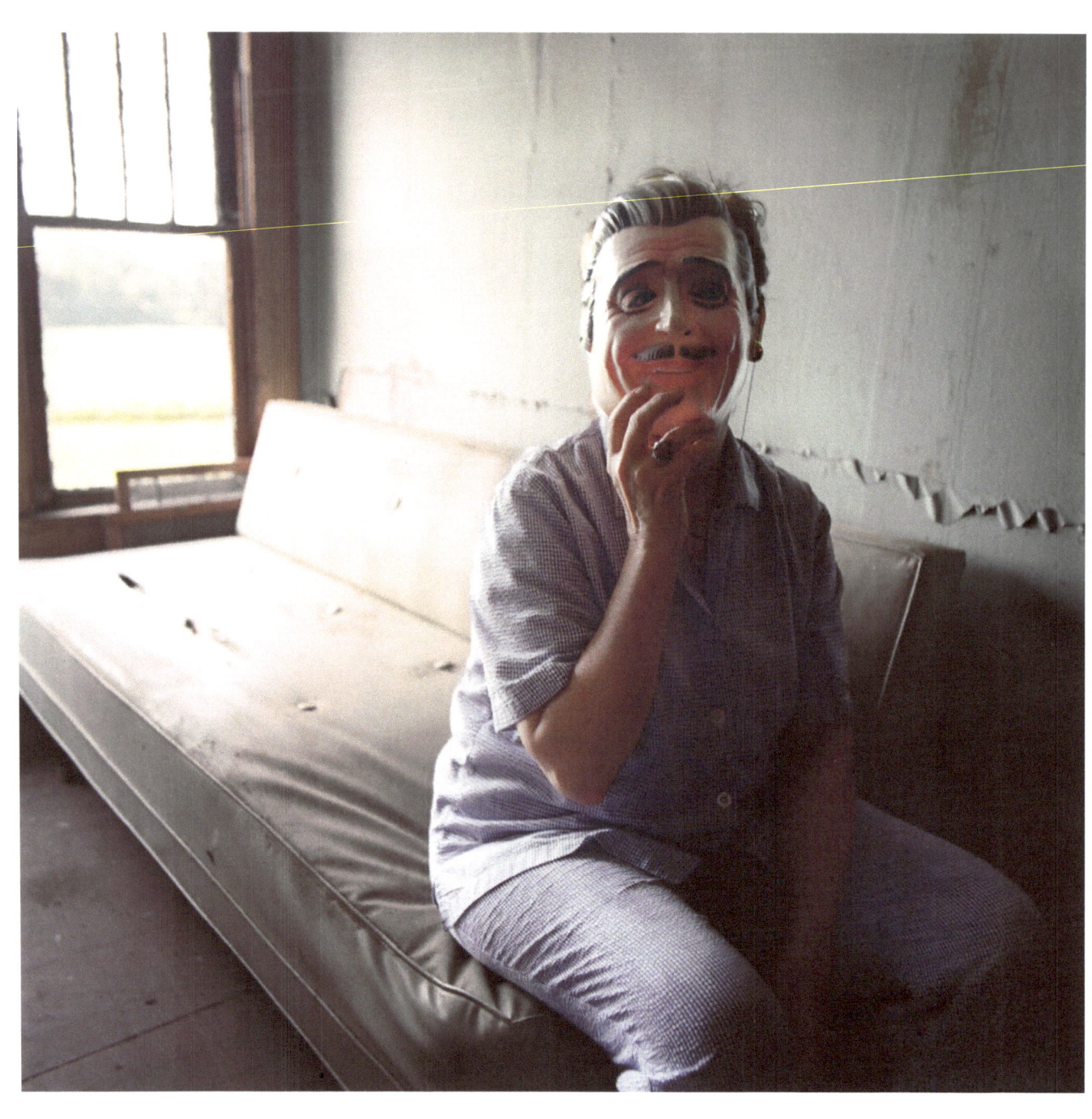

"Mom with Mask"
Piper Robbins

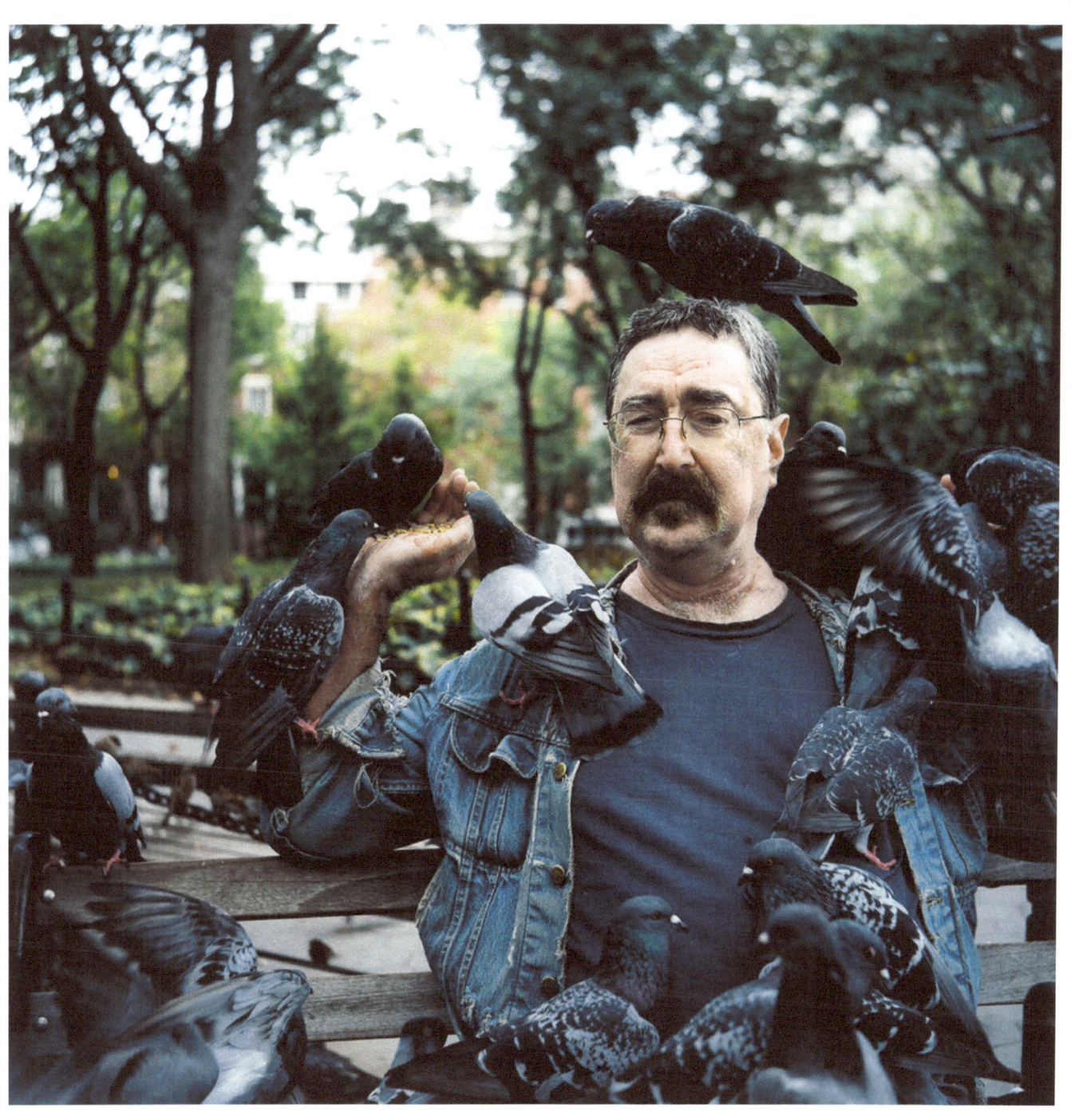

"OH YEAH!!!"
Piper Robbins

# Martin DelCarpio

aka M. is a music artist with the soul of a dreamer. With the vital help of music producers, he has been able to record a couple of records. The official first one released in 2007 is called In Absentia produced by Little Pioneer which is a record that has a sonic wave of aggressive edgy beats combined with melodic sensibilities. In Absentia is a record that talks about a time of personal struggle, a time of questioning virtue and a time of real isolation.

Martin Del Carpio then recorded a Spanish language record entitled Pequeno Pionero with Little Pioneer released in 2008. It has been a dream of his to record Latin songs but with his own singular approach. A lot of inspiration for this record came from listening to many Latin artists from the 60's and 70's. Tropic Of Capricorn recorded once again with Little Pioneer was released in 2010. It's an EP that came about spontaneously. If anything, it's a project that brought Martin Del Carpio to the notion of wanting to record more straight forward songs.

In 2011, Martin Del Carpio worked with British music producer Jamie Muffett. What came about from those recording sessions were more organic songs with a few edgy alternative tracks thrown in for good measure. The album entitled X has been officially released in late 2012. In 2013, a new album entitled Godard has been released. It's a more "soundtracky" kind of record.

martindelcarpio.bandcamp.com

reverbnation.com/martindelcarpio

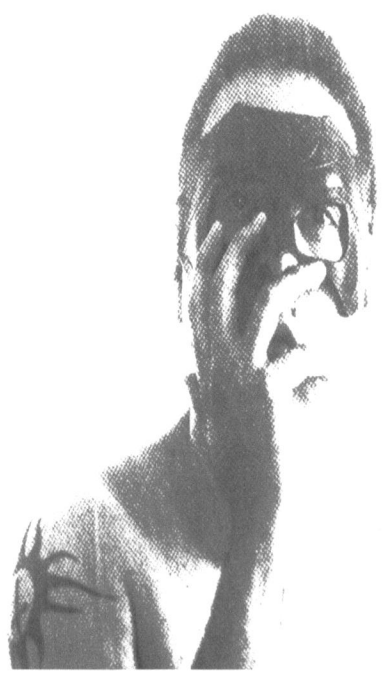

"Murmur of the Heart"
Martin DelCarpio

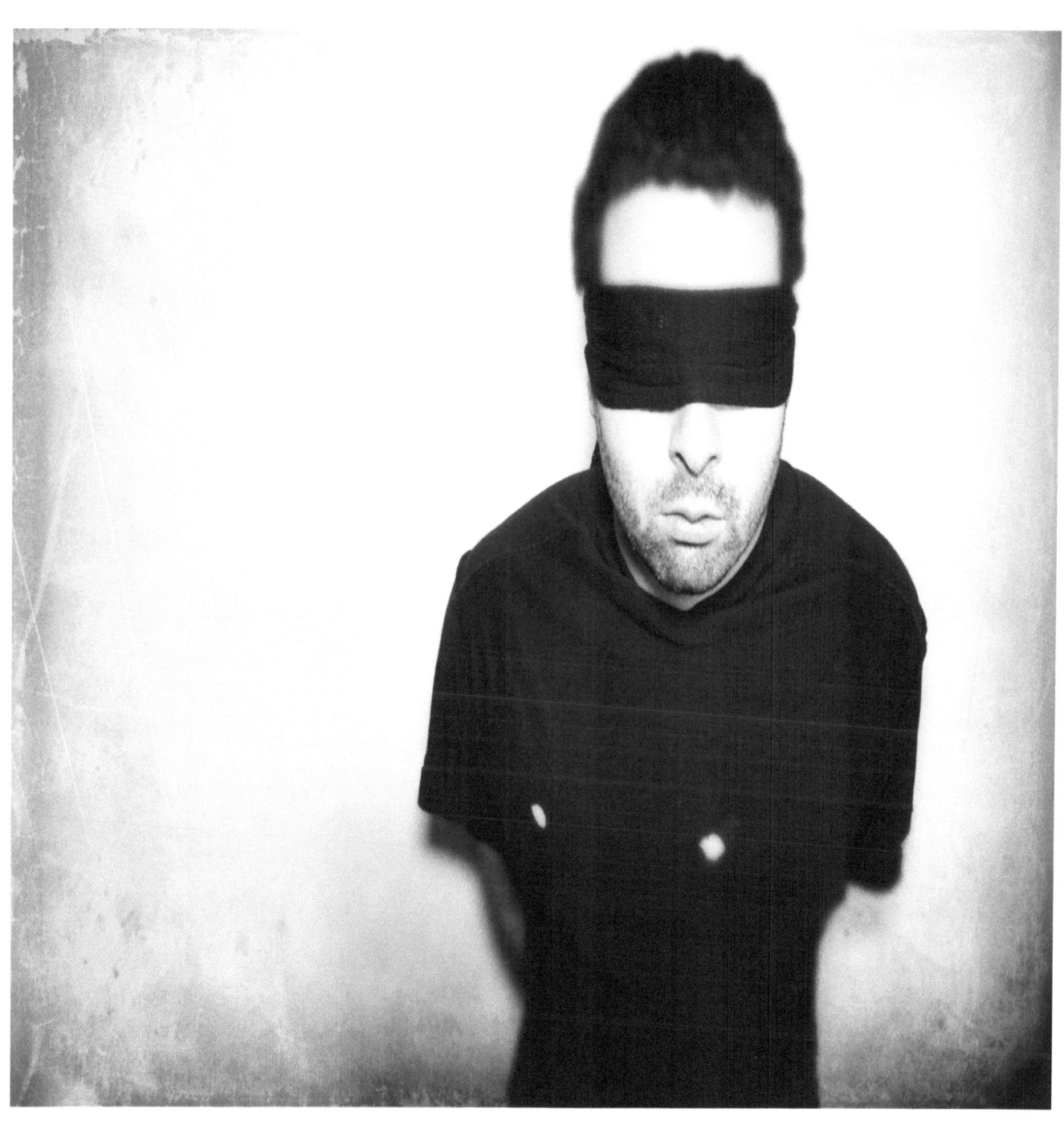

"Year Zero"
Martin DelCarpio

# SUBMIT YOUR ART to MACABRE

We are always looking for new art to include in future issues. To submit your artwork for consideration to be published in Macabre Art Magazine, please follow the requirements below:

## REQUIREMENTS:

*To submit photos of your artwork for consideration, please make sure it is 300dpi or higher and in jpeg form, and the largest size possible.

*There are no fees to submit your work and you may submit up to 10 different pieces.

*All files submitted must be labeled with last name, then first initial, then name of artwork. Example: SmithJ_graveyard.jpeg

*A completed copy of the Release Form  must be scanned and emailed with photos.

* A short bio 1-3 paragraphs long, with website, link or contact info you want to publish.

**Email 300dpi PHOTOS, RELEASE, BIO and CONTACT INFO to:**

MacabreMagazine@gmail.com

# RELEASE FORM

Grant. For consideration which I acknowledge, I consent to email photographs of my artwork, and grant to Macabre Art Magazine ("Company") and Company's assigns, licensees and successors the right to copy, reproduce, and use all or a portion of the photographs for incorporation in the following work, "Macabre - An Art Collection to Make Your Hair Stand on End" compiled by Lora Mercado (the "Work").

I permit the use of all or a portion of the photograph(s) in the Work in all forms and media including advertising and related promotion throughout the world and in perpetuity. I grant the right to use my name in connection with all uses of the photograph(s) and waive the right to inspect or approve use of my photograph(s) as incorporated in the Work.

Release. I release Company and Company's assigns, licensees and successors from any claims that may arise regarding the use of the photograph(s) including any claims of defamation, invasion of privacy, or infringement of moral rights, rights of publicity or copyright. I acknowledge that I have no ownership rights to the Work.

No compensation, monetary or otherwise will be given to contributors of the Work. All contributors will receive recognition in the book for their art and retain copyrights to their photo to use elsewhere without restriction.

Photograph(s) will not be used for any other purpose than promotion of, or publication in Work.

Company is not obligated to utilize the rights granted in this Agreement.

I have read and understood this agreement and I am over the age of 18. This Agreement expresses the complete understanding of the parties.

_____ Place an X in the line to AGREE to the terms of this contract.


_____
Artist Signature - By filling this form out electronically you are agreeing to this release.


_____
Artist Name


_____
Artist Address


Date_____